REAL AND APPARENT TRICOLA IN
HEBREW PSALM POETRY

BY

SIGMUND MOWINCKEL

Avhandlinger utgitt av Det Norske Videnskaps-Akademi i Oslo
II. Hist.-Filos. Klasse 1957. No. 2

WIPF & STOCK · Eugene, Oregon

Wipf and Stock Publishers
199 W 8th Ave, Suite 3
Eugene, OR 97401

Real and Apparent Tricola in Hebrew Psalm Poetry
By Mowinckel, Sigmund
Copyright©1957 by The Estate of Sigmund Mowickel
ISBN 13: 978-1-61097-915-3
Publication date 2/15/2012
Previously published by I Kommisjon Hos H. Aschehoug & Co., 1957

CONTENTS

The text-critical sigla are those of Biblia Hebraica, ed. R. Kittel, Editio tertia = BHK; TM means the Massoretic text. As the aime of this enquiry is not a linguistic one, nor to study the finer detais of metrics, a very simplifyed system of transcription has been used, not differentiating between the Begadkefats, except p and f, and not indicating the quantity of the vowels. An ^{æ}, ^{e} etc. indicate the metrical elision of the shewa-vowel. The false chatef-vovels are mostly left out of concideration.

1

In his paper on «The Psalm of Habakkuk» (*Studies in Old Testam. Prophecy*, Edinburg 1950, pp. 1ff), Professor W. F. Albright has a paragraph on the «repetitive or climactic parallelism» in the O. T. In many of these cases he thinks he has to do with «tricolic» verses («periodes,» «Perioden» in the terminology of Sievers). Tricolic verses M. Tsevat also finds among the samples in the somewhat different list of verses with repetitive parallelism; see his *Study of the Language of the Biblical Psalms* (JBL Monograph Series Vol. IX, Philadelphia 1955), p. 113, n. 266. Neither of them are speaking of poems of a tricolic structure throughout, but of occurences of isolated tricola in bicolic poems.

I have made some observations on the question in *Studia Orientalia Joanni Pedersen Septuagenario Dicata* (Hauniae 1953), pp. 252f; s. also my *Offersang og Sangoffer*, Oslo 1951, p. 608, n. 35. — Here I want to take up the problem of tricolic verses more in detail.

In my opinion, the tricolic structure of Hebrew verses is a much rarer phenomenon than the above-mentioned scholars and many psalm commentators think, and it this I want to demonstrate in the following pages.

a) As a short introduction some lines about my opinion of Hebrew metrics, as I have put it in «Zum Problem der hebräischen Metrik», *Bertholet-Festschrift*, Tübingen 1950, pp. 379ff; «Zur hebräischen Metrik II», *Studia Theologica* VII, 1953, pp. 54ff; «Metrischer Aufbau und Textkritik, an Ps. 8 illustriert», *Studia Orientalia Ioanni Pedersen*, Hauniae (Copenhagen) 1953, pp. 250ff; «Der metrische Aufbau von Jes. 62, 1—12 und die neuen sogen. ʿKurzverse'», *ZATW* 65, 1953, pp. 167ff; «Die Metrik bei Jesus Sirach», *StTh* XI, 1955, pp. 137ff; «Marginalien zur hebräischen Metrik», *ZATW* 68, 1956, pp. 97ff. See also my *Offersang og Sangoffer*, Oslo 1951, pp. 418ff.

The basic rhythm of Hebrew verses is the jambic, eventually with syncope

$$x \stackrel{/}{-} x \stackrel{/}{-} x \stackrel{/}{-} x \stackrel{/}{-}, \quad \text{evtl.}$$
$$x \stackrel{\sim}{-} \stackrel{/}{-} x \stackrel{/}{-} x \stackrel{/}{-}$$

Variation of the jambic structure through intermingled anapaests is rather common.

The normal (basic) smallest metrical unity — the «pedes» apart — is the «colon» (in Albright's terminology; Sievers: «Reihe») of four «pedes» (beats). The colon does not, however, as a rule appear alone, but (almost) always as bicola, or (more seldom) tricola (Sievers: «Doppelreihe» oder «Periode»). — This is due to a poetical principle, which is per se a stylistic phenomenon, not a metrical, but which is, however, of fundamental importance even for the metrics, the law of the «thought rhyme» (Lowth: parallelismus membrorum). This is again a species of the «law of duality», a common psychological-esthetical-stylistical «law», which in Hebrew poetry is so fundamental that even in such «verses» where the real thought rhyme (synonymic and antithetic parallelism) has disintegrated, it still lives as a merely formal principle, the so-called «synthetic parallelism».[1]

The caesura between the two cola almost always coincides with the grammatical and logical pause; enjambment, however, does occur, both between the two cola of a bicolon and between two bicola (seldom).

This means in fact, that the units of which a Hebrew poem is built up, normally is not the colon, but the bicolon (evtl. tricolon). This ought to be seen even from the terminology. The expressions

---

[1] S. *Stud. Orient. Joanni Pedersen dic.* pp. 250ff; *Offersang og Sangoffer* p. 425ff; *ZATW* 68, pp. 100ff. — The fundamental importance of the thought rhyme for Hebr. poetry has also been stressed by G. B. Gray, *Forms of Hebrew Poetry*, London 1915, and Th. H. Robinson, «Some Principles of Hebrew Metrics», *ZATW* 54, 1936, pp. 28ff; «Basic Prinsiples of Hebrew Poetic Form», *Bertholetfestschrift*, pp. 438ff.

«colon» and «bicolon» are in so far not very happy. The true nature of Hebrew poetry is better expressed by the terms «*stichos*» (stich) for «bicolon» and «*hemistich*» for «colon».

The normal colon (hemistich) is not, as Sievers has intended, a tripodic, but a quadrupodic, four beats to a colon. The normal bicolon is a 4 + 4 stichos («periode»), which I call the «*Mashal metre*» because of its regular use in the wisdom poetry. Sievers's «Sechser», «Siebener», «umgekehrter Siebener» are all of them wrongly scanned normal Mashal bicola (sometimes, however seldom, the logical and metrical caesura do not coincide).

Sievers distinguishes between «Doppeldreier» (3 + 3-bicola) and «Doppelvierer» (4 + 4-bicola). This distinction is illusory; they are all 4 + 4 beat stichoi (bicola). The difference between Sievers's two types is, that his «Doppelvierer», mostly, are dipodic, and his «Doppeldreier» not infrequently, monopodic four-beat bicola; very often two beats are represented by a single word, e. g. *mirúšálém*. This dipodic verse pattern is often mistaken for a 2 beat bicolon (stich), it is, however, a 4 beat colon (hemistich), which again is a part of a 4 + 4 beat bicolon (stich). A 2 beat colon does not exist in Hebrew poetry. This statement is but a necessary consequence of the fact that the thought rhyme is fundamental in this poetry, and that the thought rhyme is one between two cola, not between parts of a colon; so the thought rhyme can tell us where the colon begins and ends. Thus e. g. 29:1 proves that the first colon (hemistich) of this psalm is not the dipody *hâbu-l-yhwh*, but the double dipody *hâbu-l-yhwh bene 'elim*, followed by a second double dipody *hâbu-l-yhwh kâbod wâ'oz*, the two making a normal 4 + 4 beat stichos with thought rhyme (parallelismus membrorum).

A brachycatalectic offshot to the Mashal bicolon is the *Qinah*. This is not, as Budde, Sievers and the majority of the scholars think, a 3 + 2 beat bicolon (stichos, verse), but a 4 + 3 beat (jambic) bicolon.

As an illustration of the common Hebrew verse types, I give some examples. Circumflex designs syncope.

Dipodic four beat bicola (stichoi):

> *hâbú-l- yahwǽ bené 'elím*
> *hâbú-l-yahwǽ kâbód wâ'óz* (29:1).

'attá báqá'tá ma'yán wánáḥal,
　'attá hobáštá nahªrót 'etán (74:15).
yahwǽ málák yirgezú 'ammím
　yošéb kerubím tánúg hǽ árs (99:1).
'odǽ yahwǽ bekól libbí
　'asápperá kol-níflotǽká (9:2).
'asápperá šim'ká l-'ǽháy
　bĕtók qáhál 'ăhállelǽká (22:23).
çidqáteká kehái're-'él
　mišpáteká tehóm rabbá (36:7).
goyyim horáštá wattíṭṭá'ém
　táró'¹ l'ummím watt'šálleḥém (44:3).

In the last four examples a dipody is represented by one «sense bearing» word only.

Monopodic four beat bicola:

'ašré hǽ'íš 'asêr² ló'
　hálák bedǽrǽk réšá'ím³ (1:1).
wekól-'ašǽr ya'śǽ yaçlíḥ,
　ló' kén háréšá'ím [lo'kén, G] (1:3c 4a)⁴.
kí tif'ǽrǽt 'uzzánu 'áttá⁵
　bir'çóneká tárúm qarnénu (89:18).
hémmá káre'ú wenáfálu
　wa'náḥnu qámnu wanniť odád (20:9).
wa'ªní kim''át nátúy raglí
　ke'áyin šúppekú 'ašuráy (73:2).
kí ḥamát 'ádám todǽká
　šerîṭ⁶ ḥémaṭ[ó] taḥgór (76:11).
libbâm⁶ ló' nákón 'immó
　weló' nǽ'ªmû bíb'ritó (78:37).

¹ tr' here from √⁻ r'' = rçç.
² On the syncope see StTh VII pp. 66ff.
³ On the possibility of giving a shewa vowel metrical accent see StTh VII, p. 57, and especially ZATW 68, pp. 117ff.
⁴ Antithetic parallelism. The verse division in TM is logically correct, but metrically wrong. See below p. 23.
⁵ NB the accentuation in TM.
⁶ On the syncope see StTh VII pp. 66ff.

ki rûḥ yăʿbor-bó weʾnǽnnu
    welô' yakkirǽnnu ʿód meqomó (104:16).

Qinah verses (stichoi, «bicola»):

'ekă ydšebá bădăd
    hăʿír rabbáti ʿám (Lam. 1:1).

hăyú săræhă kᵉáyyălím
    lô'-máçe'ú mirʿæ (Lam. 1:6).

binᵉ ʤól ʿammăh beyăd săr
    weʾén ʿozêr lăh (Lam. 1:7).

billăʿ yahwæ welô' hămál
    'et kól-nᵉ'ót yăʿᵃqób (Lam. 2:2).

míšpeʤé yahwæ 'æmæt
    çádequ yahdăw (Ps. 19:10).

'im¹ táhănæ ʿálăy mahanæ
    lô' yirá' libbí,

'im¹ táqúm ʿálăy milhámá
    bezót 'ani boʤéᵃh (Ps. 27:3).

má tištóhăhí naʤší
    umá tæhᵃmí ʿálăy,

hohili-l-yahwæ ki ʿód 'odænnu
    yešuʿát pănăy welohăy (43:5).²

When the jambi can be varied through syncope and inter-mingled with anapaests, it goes without saying that some verses *can* be scanned in different ways, e. g. both as Mashal and as Qinah verses. Which, in the definite case, is the correct reading depends on the structure of the poem in question as a totality. This is a phenomenon common to the poetry of very many languages, English, Danish, German, Norwegian, Swedish etc.

Budde, Sievers and many others think that *their* Qinah (3 + 2) often may be varied by a «shortened Qinah», a supposed 2 + 2 beat bicolon (stichos). These supposedly two-beat verses are, in fact, nothing but wrongly-scanned regular Qinoth.³ E. g.

---

¹ As in all other poetry the regularly unaccented «small words» sometimes have the metrical accent and sometimes not. See *ZATW* 68, pp. 115ff.

² Regular Qinah, against Gunkel (*Die Psalmen*, p. 12), who believes v. 5b to be a «final verse in a different metre».

³ See *StTh* VII pp. 82f.

yebóšu wéyikkálemú | mebáqqěšé nafší (35 : 4a),
hásdeká wa'mítteká | támîd yíççerúni (40 : 12b).

Having recognized the fundamental jambic structure of the Hebrew verse, it goes without saying that Sievers's «Siebener» (4 + 3) and «Umgekehrter Siebener» (3 + 4) are nothing but wrongly-scanned normal Mashal bicola.[1]

As a variant of his «Doppeldreier« (3 + 3) Sievers considers what he calls the «Sechser» (2 + 2 + 2); there does not exist any such «Sechser». They are partly wrongly-scanned Qinah verses, e. g.

bárúk yahwæ šælló' netánánu | tárf le-šinnehæm (124:6)[2].

Mostly, they are regular Mashal bicola, with enjambment, however, between the two cola, as in 1:1 (see above p. 8), or 8:1:

yahwæ 'ªdoné ιu má 'addír | šiměká 'al-kól há'áræç[3]

As already mentioned, the bicolon (stich) (with thought rhyme), not the single colon (hemistich), is the normal form of Hebrew verses.

The artistic law of duality, however, is not only at work within the single bicolon, making a thought rhyme out of the two cola of the «verse» but it tends to bind also two and two bicola together to a «stanza» (strophe), the basic or normal stanza of Hebrew poetry. The thought rhyme, the «parallelism» of the two bicola of a stanza is, however, often less strong than between the two cola of the bicolon; but the tendency to build a logical — and formal! — connection between two and two bicola, is rather fundamental.

This we can most easily observe from the Qinah verses.

As there normally is not sufficient place here in the second colon for a full synonymous or antithetic parallelism, evolution has led to the result that mostly not two cola (hemistichs), but two bicola (stichs) build a thought rhyme; the second, shorter, colon of the Qinah verse is mostly not a «parallel» variation of the first, but its syntactical and logical continuation. Thus the Qinah tends to the building of small «stanzas» of two stichs (bicola), the simple «basic stanza» of Hebrew poetry, the distich, to speak in the classical terminology.

---

[1] See *ibid*. p. 83.
[2] See *ibid* p. 83.
[3] See *ibid*. p. 83f, and *Johs. Pedersen - Festskrift*, pp. 254f.

The same tendency, however, we observe in the Mashal metre as well: two and two bicola hang logically and formally nearer together and make the basic «stanza». This is almost always the case in the Psalms — except where we have to do with larger and more artistically built up stanzas.[1]

b) One thing should, however, never be forgotten when dealing with Hebrew metrics and Psalm exegesis: the uncertainty of the sound text. This may sound disrespectful in the ears of the modern idolaters of TM, but nevertheless, it is true.

Two circumstances should be taken into consideration here:

First, the transmission of the text. This was originally, and perhaps for centuries, oral. Slips of memory are then unavoidable; a verseline or two, even a whole stanza, may have been forgotten, or displaced; the different modern transcriptions of old Norwegian folk songs prove that we have not to do with possibilities only, but with facts. Later on, the psalms were written down, probably gradually, and copied and copied again. No one can imagine that this repeated copying of unvocalized texts can have taken place without all those varied mistakes which can and must happen. That we here, too, are not speaking of possibilities only, but of facts, the doublets in the Psalter (14 = 53; 70 = 40:14—18; 108 = 75:8—12 + 60:7—14; 18 = 2 Sam. 22) suffice to prove. Comparing Ps. 18 with 2 Sam. 22, we very soon realize, that there are not many lines without variations, among them both omissions and secondary additions. The end of the history of transmission was the revision of the text by the learned men of the Jewish congrega-

---

[1] See the Author's *Offersang og Sangoffer*, pp. 430ff, and below, Additional Note. See also J. A. Montgomery, «Stanza-Formation in Hebrew Poetry», *JBL* 64, 1945, pp. 379ff. — It is astonishing to see how little e.g. A. Weiser, *Die Psalmen I—II* (*Das Alte Testament Deutsch* 14—15), Göttingen 1955, has to say about stanzas in the psalms. As far as I can see, he speaks about «stanzas» («Strophen») — mostly not quite regular ones — only in connection with Pss. 1, 2, 6, 16, 42/43, 46, 59, 65, 140. To judge from the way he prints the lines in his translation, he seems to find regular stanzas only in Pss. 42/43, 46, 114, 127, 130 and 139:17—24, more irregular ones in 22, 24, 99, 118, 125, 146.

tion and the authorization of a certain type of text. The «Urtext» can never be reconstructed with certainty, and even if it could, it would certainly be found hampered with errors already from the oral stage of transmission.

Secondly, we must not forget that the psalms are cultic songs. They have been used in the liturgies of living worship throughout centuries. During this long period both religious ideas and elements of the liturgy have changed; they have had their history and a historical evolution. This includes at least the possibility of revisions of the psalms as well, in accordance with the change and modifications of the religious ideas during the interchange of time. I know no Christian hymnal that has not had its revisions.

All these things may have — and have certainly had their influence on the form of the psalms.

One might ask: if this be the condition of the text, should not then metrical investigation be impossible? The answer to this is: as long as the transmitters and copyists are still conscious of the rules and forms of their national poetry, this will keep the alterations and variants of the «text» — oral or written — within certain limits, just those limits drawn by the metrical rules — of course, not always, and not without offence against the rules. A word may be changed by a synonym; an article, a nota accusativi, a relative pronoun or the like may be put in, etc., but still we are within the area of the possible metrical freedom. That the transmission, in the main, is true, is seen e. g. from a single trait as the archaistic poetic omission of the article, still preserved in the text, although the Massoretes, in accordance with the linguistic usage of their own time, have tried to put it in again through the interpunction wherever it was possible, i. e. especially in words with the enclitic particles *be*, *ke*, *le*[1]. — So it should not be impossible from the point of view of metrics, to recognize a gloss, a doublet and a lacuna.

This knowledge of the old poetical rules has lasted long. Jesus Sirach still keeps the old metrical and poetical rules[2]. The Qumrān Hodayoth and the Psalms of Solomon have forgotten them, at least they do not follow them.

[1] See Mowinckel, *Der Achtundsechzigste Psalm*, pp. 15f.

[2] See the Author's article in *StTh XI*, pp. 137ff.

2.

No one has ever since the beginning of the exploration of Hebrew metrics denied the *existence of a tricolic metre*. The question is, how the tricola, the tripartite stichs, are used.

Undoubtedly there are poems of a tricolic structure. There are also poems where a shorter or longer section is built up in that way. My first thesis is now just this, that in those cases the whole psalm, or the whole definite section in question, is thoroughly and regularly built up of tricola. We have to do with *poems, or definite sections of a poem, of an entirely tricolic structure*.

a) *Tricolic in their entirety* are the following psalms:

Ps. 93. In v. 5 we certainly have to read *'addir mim-mišběre yåm;* v. 2b is a little too short; T adds *'el*, and a word like this (evtl. *'ælohim* or *yhwh*), must be supplemented; s. BHK. At all events, the tricolic structure is quite obvious in the vv. 1b—2, v. 3, v. 4, v. 5. This being the case, one is entitled to believe that the poet intended to make a psalm in regular tricolic form, and that some words have been lost in v. la through homoioteleuton; before *'oz* we may safely add *hådår wehod, yhwh,* cpr. 96:6; 104:1.

Tricolic in its entirety is also **Ps. 138.** There can be no doubt that the plus in v. 1 given in many mss. and by G: *yhwh,* and *ki šåma'ti 'imre pi,* is original. The same is the case with the plus of G in v. 3; 1. *beyom qeråtikå [yhwh] / wattěmåher watta'aneni /tarbeni benafši 'oz.* Thus the tricolic form in vv. 1, 3 is restituted. The thought rhyme (parall. membr.) shows that v. 5a must be connected with v. 4, and v. 5b with v. 6. V. 2 provisionally left alone, the tricola run as follows: vv. 1; 3; 4—5a; 5b—6; 7; 8. This far-reaching regularity justifies the supposition that even v. 2 in its original form must have been tricolic. In fact, v. 2 *has* the outer form of a tricolon — against the division of the lines in BHK; the reason for this division, however, is the fact that both 2b and 2c are much too long for a single colon respectively. There can, however, be no doubt that the text of v. 2 is damaged; v. 2c gives no sense; *'imråtækå* has no syntactical connection with the preceding words. Commentators have sometimes considered *'mtk* 2b and *'mrtk* 2c as dittographies, and BHK proposes to delete *we'al 'amittekå* 2b, thus reducing the over-length of the verse. Here, however, the question of stanzas comes in. From v. 4 on, two and two tricola make a logically defined stanza: vv. 4—6 and 7—8. By reducing v. 2 to one tricolon, we should in v. 1—3 have a stanza of 3 tricola. Well, that might perhaps be accepted. But here the rules of composition of the thanksgiving psalm[1] announce themselves. The thanksgiving psalm begins ordinarily with a general expression of the worshipper's intention to thank and praise God — or with a general statement of His praiseworthiness — and then follows «the record» (the narrative) about the worshipper's experiences, his distress and his salvation; this part of the psalm has the form of a motivation of the introductory statement, and accordingly, is often connected with this by a *ki*. This *ki* announces a new section of the psalm. In the transmitted text this *ki* is found before v. 2c, which, then, impossibly can be a third colon of a tripartite stich, a «long verse» (a tricolon). We cannot, therefore, avoid the conclusion, that v. 2 originally must have made 2 tricola, and that the healing of the corrupted text here, as so often is not found by deleting, but, on the contrary by supplementing some lost words.[2] It seems justifiabel to put in a *yhwh* behind *šiměkå* in v. 2b, and to supplement v. 2c (from *ki* on) after 119:38, reading:

> *ki higdaltå ʿal-kol* (or: *hak-kol*) *šiměkå*
> [*haqimotå leʿabdekå*] *ʾimråtækå,*

and then something like:

> *higgadtå ʾæt darke çidqåtækå.*

Tricolic is undoubtedly also the original form of **Ps. 100**. V. 1b is, of course ,to be connected with v. 2, as BHK shows. Only v. 5 is too short; but in accordance with the style of the hymn of praise, where the last stanza (or verse) takes up again the introitus with its call to doxology,[3] it seems to be legitimate to supplement v. 5 after 106:1 and read *hodu leyhwh, ki ṭob,/yahwh leʿolåm ḥasdo/ weʿad -dor etc.*

---

[1] See H. Gunkel-J. Begrich, *Einleitung in die Psalmen*, Göttingen 1933, pp. 265ff; S. Mowinckel, *Offersang og Sangoffer*, pp. 284ff.

[2] See below §§ 4 (pp. 31ff), 7c (pp. 56ff).

[3] See Gunkel-Begrich, *Einleitung i. d. Pss.* pp. 33f, 38, 57f.

Ps. 45 also seems to be tricolic, except the last bicolic stanza, vv. 17—18. In v. 5 the three first words have to be connected with v. 4 (del. however, *wahadåreká*, BHK); v. 5c (*wetoreká* etc.) belongs together with v. 6; v. 8a has to be connected with v. 7, and v. 9a with v. 8b, c; v. 9b with v. 10; v. 12a with v. 11, and v. 12b with v. 13; v. 15a with v. 14; the rest of v. 15 makes together with v. 16 the last tricolon.

b) In other cases the *tricola* occur only in a distinct *section of a psalm*. As a rule, the section with the differing metre is not an arbitrarily or at ransom chosen part of the poem, but a definite section of the whole, thematically and stilistically making a smaller unit within the composition.

So it is in **24:7—10**, the last scene of the dramatical procession liturgy,[1] before the temple gate, where a) access is demanded for the King of Glory; b) the doorkeepers ask who is this King of Glory, and c) the participents in the procession answer by shouting out the name of the coming God: Yahweh Seba'oth. Corresponding to these 3 points of content, we also have the tricolic form of the «long verse» (stich). Two «long verses», one for the request of opening the doors, and one for the question and the answer, make a stanza; the repetition of the whole scene gives another. It ought to be observed that within the tricolon all the three cola have a relation of «parallelism» to each other; in the first tricolon two synonymous membra for the request itself, and one giving the reason for the demand for opening the doors; in the second, one membrum for the question and two synonymous ones for the answer:

> Raise your arches, O ye gates
> raise yourselves, ye ancient doors,
> that the King of Glory may come in.

> Who is the King of Glory?
> Yahweh, strong and mighty,
> Yahweh, mighty in battle.

---

[1] On this psalm and its cultic situation see *Offersang og Sangoffer*, pp. 176, 190; 329ff.

In the second stanza the two last cola vary the answer giving the full cult name of the God:

> Yahweh the God of hosts,
> He is the King of Glory.

In the national psalm of lamentation[1] **Ps. 60** the lament and the prayer in the first and the last part of the psalm, vv. 3—7 and 11—14, are composed in the regular 4 + 4 beat Mashal metre, but the divine oracle in the second part, vv. 8—10, is built up of three tricola (4 + 4 + 4). The shift of the metre is of course due to the shift in content. — The tricolic oracle has been taken up in **108: 8—10**.

In the national psalm of lamentation **77** the first part vv. 2—13 consists of four regular stanzas in Mashal metre, three bicola to the stanza. The second part vv. 14—21, a hymnic description of Yahweh's wonderful deeds in old times, is tricolic (4 + 4 + 4), in short lapidare clauses in the traditional hymnic style. V. 15a must be connected with v. 14, and 15b with v. 16 (against TM andBHK). — The shift of the metre corresponds to the shift of content and emotion. In this case the author may have taken up a part of an older hymn of praise. At all events the psalm now is fragmentary; the mentioning of the leadership of Moses and Ahron can only have been meant as an introduction to a more detailed description of the miracles of salvation during the sojourn in the wilderness; with the abrupt v. 21 neither the actual psalm nor the assumed older poem can have ended. So it might be most probable that even v. 21 originally was a tricolon, although it cannot be denied that the quotation of the older psalm may have ended with v. 20, and that the author then continued the description in the bicolic metre of the first part of his poem.

We have two real tricola in **79:1—2**, the beginning of the «lament» proper in this national psalm of lamentation. Why only these two at the head of a psalm, the corpus of which is in regular bicolic Mashal metre? Probably to give these lines a special weight:

---

[1] See *Offersang*, pp. 192ff; on Ps. 60. pp. 204, 219, 313f, 338f.

even thy own sanctuary the heathens have defiled, the slain bodies of thine own saints they have thrown as food to the wild beasts! Mentioning this horrible fact, the poet has felt that what he had to say, could not be said in two sentences only; the tricola will stress the lament and thus make the appeal the more urgent.

Also **97:7—10**, the tricolic middle section of a bicolic «hymn of enthronement»,[1] *may* have been a part of an older poem, taken up by the author of the actual psalm.

Tricolic is also the refrain in **99:5,9**. I take it for granted that v. 5 has to be filled up after v. 9; we thus get two stanzas, 4 bicola + refrain to each stanza.

— In the wisdom poetry, too, we sometimes see the tricolic form, s. *Prov. 30:15—16*, even in isolated sentences among bicola only, s. *Prov. 30:20, 33*. That is no cause for wonder, however, as the isolated sentence is the original form of the wisdom poetry.

c) The above-mentioned psalms and sections of a psalm teach us some-thing important about the *nature of the genuine tricolon*. The main rule is here, as it is in the bicolon, that all the three cola (membra) show a more or less exact parallelism between each other. The parallelism is very often of the climactic or repetitive sort.

> The floods lifted up, Yahweh,
> > the floods lifted up their voice,
> > > the floods lifted up their waves (93:3).

> More than the voice of the many waters,
> > mightier than the breakers of the ocean
> > > is Yahweh mighty in high (93 : 4).

> The waters saw thee, O God,
> > the waters saw thee and quivered,
> > > the depths of the ocean shivered (77:17).

Even without «repetition» there can be a full «identical parallelism» between the three cola:

[1] See Mowinckel, *Psalmenstudien* II, Oslo 1922; *Offersang*, pp. 118ff.

Yahweh has become king, has clothed himself in majesty,
    Yahweh has clothed himself [in splendour and dignity,
        Yahweh] has girded himself with strength (93:1a).

Shout praise to Yahweh, all the earth,
    join his service now with gladness,
        enter his presence with songs of praise! (100:1–2).

So even in 100:4 and 100:5. — Or with a slight nuance:

O God, the pagans have invaded thy preserve,
    thy sacred shrine they have profaned,
        Jerusalem have they laid in ruins (79:1).

Yahweh 'loves those who hate' evil,
    he preserves the lives of his devotees,
        he delivers them from the hand of the wicked (97:10).

For thou, Yahweh, art the Most High,
    thou art exalted above all the earth,
        thou art 'terrible' over all the gods (97:9).

In other cases the 2nd and the 3rd colon contain a further explanation of the thought expressed in the 1st (or 2nd):

Thou hast established[1] the world unshakable,
    from then thy throne stands firm,
        from eternity thou art [God] (93:1b—2).

The poet speaks of the *creation*, the *establishing* (*tikken*) of the world, now re-experienced in the cult; since *that time*[2] (*me'åz*) even Yahweh's throne and kingdom have been firmly *established* (*nåkon*), and so he has proved to be (the only real) God form *eternity* (i. e., the beginning of time). — See also above p. 15 on 24:7ff.

The parallelism between the three cola is clear even in 77:20:

[1] Read *tikken*, Verss. 75:4, BHK.
[2] Or: «from old», Moffatt.

> Thy way was through the sea,
>   thy path through the great waters,
>   although thy footsteps were not seen.

Here v. a and b build an «identical parallelism», and v. c adds in antithetic form an explanation of Yahweh's wonderful «way» and «path».

The 2nd colon may even give an addition to the idea or picture in the 1st. V. a and b then build a socalled «synthetical parallelism», i. e. they build no real thought rhyme, only the duality of the cola is kept. V. b may even be the syntactic continuation of a:

> I will thank thee, Yahweh, with my whole heart
>   for thou hast heard the words of my mouth,
>   before the Gods I will sing praise unto thee (138:1G).

> All the kings of the earth shall praise thee, Yahweh,
>   when they hear the words of my mouth,
>   yea, they shall sing of the ways of Yahweh (138:4f).

Here v. a and b belong together as a unit, and c is the «parallel» to a—b, formally especially to a. — In the first case the law of parallelism is at work even between a and b: «I vill thank thee» «for thou hast heard»; «with my whole heart» «the words of my mouth».

In 79:2 v. c builds the shorter parallel to a + b:

> They have flung the corpses of thy servants
>   as food to the beards under the heaven,
>   the flesh of thy devotees to the wild beasts.

See also 97:7, where a and c are parallel, while b gives an explanation of the «worshippers of images», in a.

It may also happen that a and b build the thought rhyme proper, while c adds a new element, that even syntactically is connected with b:

> Zion has heard it and rejoices,
>   the towns of Judah are in joy
>   because of thy judgements, Yahweh (98:8).

The same is the case in 93 : 5:

> Thy promisses are very sure,
>> holiness becomes thy house,
>>> O Yahweh, in all eternity.

The promises given at the feast, are sure, because the Lord's
«holiness», his divine power, now dwells in the temple, where he
has taken his seat as a King.

In 77:14—15a v. b and c build the closer parallelism, both of
them explaining the content of Yahweh's «holyness» in v. a, here
= his wonderfull divine power:

> Thy way, O God, was in (i. e. it showed) sanctity!
>> Which god is so great as 'Yahweh',
>>> Thou art the God that makes wonder!

See also 60:8, where v. b and c give the word that Yahweh
has spoken:

> Yahweh has spoken in his sanctuary:[1]
>> Rejoicing I will divide up the hillside,
>>> parcel out the valley with hedgerows.[2]

In other cases again the three cola give one element respectively
of the act described:

> The clouds poured out water,
>> the skies sent out (their) voice,
>>> thine arrows also went abroad (77:18).

> In the wheels was the voice of thy thunder,
>> the lightenings lit up the world,
>>> the earth trembled and shook (77:19).

> Gilead is mine and Manasse is mine,
>> Ephraim is the helmet of my head,
>>> and Judah is my (royal) mace (60:9).

---

[1] Not: «in his holiness» (AV).

[2] «Hillside and valley» = the whole land of the enemy. *sukkot* = *besukkot*
= the hedges of briers or thornbushes around the fields, as boundaries
between the properties. The interpretation of *šekem* and *sukkot* as proper
names is impossible here.

> Moab is my wash-basin,
>> over Edom I cast out my shoe,
>>> and over Philistea 'I will' triumph (60:10).

It may also happen that all three cola only have a logical connection between each other, without building any thought rhyme at all, but they are all of them necessary for the thought that the poet wants to express. This is the case in 138:8, the last stanza of a thanksgiving psalm:

> Yahweh will lead my case to a lucky end,
>> (for) thy lovingkindness, Yahweh, never fails.
>>> Forsake not the work of thy hands!

The poet wants to end his psalm by expressing the confidence he has won through his (renewed) experience of God's never failing lovingkindness (a—b) and to round the psalm off by the prayer that God never may forsake him, but ever again «lead his case to a lucky end».

Always, however, all three cola of the tricolon, are parts of a triple thought rhyme, in so far «synonymous» as, even if one of them, no matter whether the 1st, the 2nd or the 3rd, were missing, the two remaining would make a sufficient thought rhyme, a regular parallelismus membrorum. Of course, it might then happen that the parallelism would become only a «synthetical» one, i.e. no real thought rhyme, only a double colon; as e.g. if we omit the 1st colon in 97:8. It is, however, a well-known fact that sometimes the thought rhyme has «disintegrated», and only the duality remains —just what Lowth called «synthetical parallelism», doubtless a younger «evolution» of the original identity of the cola, the simple repetition.[1]

The 3rd (or the 2nd) colon can add a new element of the picture or idea, but never a quite new idea or thought. In the real tricolon the single colon never is an independent thought of its own, e.g. neither 2:12 or 25:1—2, nor 25:5 are real tricola.

The tricolon is certainly due to a later evolution of the older bicolon, even if it occurs already in the Ugaritic poetry. — As the

---

[1] S. *ZATW* 65, p. 174; *Offersang og Sangoffer*, pp. 425f.

nature of the bicolon consists of the formal duplicity of the same thought unity, so the tricolon appears to consist of the formal triplicity of the thought. That is the case even in such a tricolon as 97:8; to the full expression of the thought belongs even the mention of at *what* Zion and the towns of Judah are rejoicing.

This close logical connexion between the three parts (cola) of a real tricolon we have to bear in mind during the following enquiry.

3.

Many scholars now think it to be a regular trait of Hebrew poetry that tricolic verses appear sporadically among the «long verses» of a poem of bicolic structure.

The question under dispute is: do such isolated sporadic tricola occur at all, and if so, to what extent? Can they be concidered a normal phenomenon of Hebrew poetry?

In this enquiry I restrict to the Psalms. The prophetic poetry is of a more improvisatory kind, where many irregularities are likely to be found.

My second thesis is now that many of the at first glance apparent tricola are only due to incorrect and fallacious interpretation in TM and/or incorrect division of the verse lines in the print of BHK and/ or in the interpretation of modern scholars.

We begin with the simplest case, **29:1—2**, which Albright (*op.cit.* p. 6) takes as «a tristich, composed of bicola with two beats to a colon.» It is seen here that when A. writes «1f», he means vv. 1—2a. — The proton pseudos is here the theory of the «two beat metre». No such metre exists in Hebrew poetry, at least not in the Psalms, see above p. 7. Albright confounds the very common dipodic structure of the Hebr. verses (s. above) with the higher metrical unity, the colon. In vv. 1—2a we have 3 four beat-cola. — The second mistake is that he separates v. 2a from 2b and connects v. 2a with v. 1 to a separate metrical unity. The verse division in TM is quite correct; 2a must be connected with 2b. The metre in v. 2b is the same as in the other three cola: a dipodic four beat colon. The line is a little longer than the other three, but *can* very well be scanned with four beats; it may, however, be, that some scribe has mistaken an original *lo* as an abbreviation of *lyhwh* and filled up the word in this way. The two cola of each bicolon build, as usual, a «thought rhyme», a parallelism, in v. 1 according to the scheme abcd abef and in v. 2, the scheme abcd ebfg, but in reality v. 2a is = 2b: they give glory to Yahweh by falling down before him in «festal attire» (Moffatt), or «in his holy court» (G). — This «stanza» vv. 1—2 is the stilistically regular «introitus» to the hymn of praise, the «call to praise God». — The corpus of the hymn begins with v. 3.

Erroneous verse division and misconception of the parallelism (thought rhyme), we have in **1:3b, 4**. The verses are not two tricola; v. 4a should be connected with v. 3c as the antithetic parallel colon: whatsoever he (i.e., the just man) does shall prosper — (but) not so the ungodly! The following verses then give the detailed explanation of this new theme. That this is the composition planned by the author, is seen from the fact that the psalm thus falls in three stanzas, each to three bicola: vv. 1—2, vv. 3—4a, vv. 4b—6.

7:7—9 in TM seem to consist of a tricolon, a bicolon, and a tricolon. BHK has seen that v. 9a belongs together with v.8, and that v. 9bc (+ *gomleni*, BHK[3]) is a normal bicolon. But in fact vv. 7c and 8a are the two parallel membra of a bicolon, and so are vv. 8b and 9a as well: the worshipper asks Yahweh to call on the *le'ummim*, «the (heavenly) princes» (= Accad. *li'mu, limu*) to come together as his tribunal vv. 7c, 8a, and then to take his seat of judgement and «judge» the worshipper, i.e. demonstrate his justice against the «nations» vv. 8b, 9a, 9bc. — The psalm then appears to be built up of 10 regular «basic stanzas», 2 bicola to the stanza. — On v. 6 see below p. 75.

A clear case is **8:2—3**, where all exegetical reasons agree that v. 3a, the three first words, must be connected with v. 2. I have discussed this question in detail in my paper «Metrischer Aufbau und Textkritik, on Ps. 8 illustriert», in *Studia Orientalia Ioanni Pedersen*, pp. 251ff.

11:1—2 are wrongly divided in TM. V. 2b, c are the two parallel cola of a bicolon. V. 2a must be connected with v. 1, giving the motivation of the call to flight in v. 1c. This motivation is then explained in the following stanza vv. 2b—3: when the wicked are ready to shoot the upright, hidden by the «darkness» and as even the foundations (of the Cosmos) seem to be destroyed, what can then the righteous do? — 5 basic stanzas. On v. 6 see below § 8d, p. 75.

Erroneous inter-punctuation we also have in **14:3 = 53:4**. V. b and c are the two parallel cola of a Qinah. V. a is a little too short for a complete Qinah, but for *sår* 53:4 reads *såg*, which is obviously an abbreviation or a fragment of a *nåsog 'åḥor* (BHK); then the Qinah in v. 3a becomes complete.

Also **14:7 = 53:7** consists of 2 bicola; new line with *bešub*; v. 7ab is to be scanned *mi yittên miççiyyón yešú'at¹-yiśrå'él*, a Qinah bicolon, as are the other stichs of this psalm. Only v. 8cd is now a Mashal bicolon. Who soever is not inclined to allow this irregularity, might guess that the original wording may have been: *yågal ya'ªqob bešimḥå*.

In **15:3,5** both the verse division and the division of the lines in the print of BHK are misleading. See below § 11.

In **17:3—5**, too, the Massorete verse division is incorrect; *bal-ya'ªbå-pi* v. 3 makes together with the two first words in v. 4a, a regular colon, parall. v. 4b, s. BHK. The two last words of v. 4 cannot be connected with the preceding words; the pious worshipper cannot say that he has «kept» the «paths of the destroyer» (*påriç*); *šåmar* means always the loyal «keeping» of the (divine) commandments and ways; the only possible object to *šåmarti* is *debar śĕfåtækå*, the Athnach must be put to *'ådåm*. BHK is, however, mistaken in connecting *'orḥot påriç* with v. 5; the worshipper cannot, of course, say that «his steps have kept close (read *tåmeku*) to the paths of the destroyer»; moreover, v. 5 is long enough for a normal bicolon. We must, therefore, suppose that something has been lost before and/or after *'orḥot påriç*. — BHK is also mistaken in printing v. 1 on one line; the verse consists of 2 normal bicola.

¹ See below p. 33 n. 1.

The massoretic interpunction in **19:15** is logically correct, but metrically incorrect. G has a *tåmid* after *lefånækå*, which is obviously original. Then the verse must be read as 2 Qinoth — the regular metre of vv. 8ff:

> yehí-l-råsôn 'ímre-pí | wehåegyón libbí,
> lefånækå yahwǽ tåmid | çurí wegô'ålí,

with «schwebende Betonung»[1] (*lefånækå*). We have here one of the rather rare cases of enjambment between the «long verses» (stichs).

27:6 is printed in BHK as 3 lines, but consists only of 2 Qinah-periods: v. a and v. b c; the latter ought to be printed as one line. The second part of v. b c is a little too long; the two verbs may be variants.

The line division **32:9** in BHK gives the impression of some sort of tricolon, tripartite verse. The verse, however, consists of 2 Qinah bicola; 9b begins with *bemætæg* etc. The whole psalm is written in Qinoth, except v. 11, where, however, *wegilu* may be a textual variant of *weharninu*, and *kol-* a later addition.

39:6c, 7a are the two parallel cola of a bicolon, that together with v. 7bc make a stanza. Read *kehæbæl* v. 6. *sælåh* must probably be replaced after v. 7.

The verses are also wrongly divided in **40:7—9**. The metre of this psalm is the Qinah.

This is, however, blurred in vv. 7b—11. In vv. 7—11 the worshipper mentions the thanksgiving he now, after being helped in his troubles, is bringing: not sacrifices of animals, but his song of praise and his witness in the congregation; he will not be silent about the justice and faithfulness of Yahweh, but proclaim it loudly, scil. in this psalm of thanksgiving. But still better is another thanksgiving: to have God's commandments in his heart, and keep them. — Here v. 7b misses its necessary logical continuation; we expect something like 51:18b. This is, however, found in v. 8a, where *hnh b'ty* has no sense in this context; we certainly have to read

---

[1] See on this metrical phenomenon *Bertholet-Festschrift*, p. 386; *StTh XI*, p. 56; *ZATW* 68, pp. 120ff.

hen hebe'ti [låk] and connect with v. 7b. The rest of v. 8 then makes a good Qinah verse continued by v. 9:

> *Then I say: In the book scroll*
> *is written concerning me (i.e., what I have to do);*
> *to do thy will is my delight, my God,*
> *thy law is within my heart.*

'*ælohay* may be deleted, making the first half of v. 9 too long.

On vv. 10—11 see below § 8b (p. 69f).

55:15—16. The psalm is built up of regular stanzas, two bicola to the stanza. V. 15c must be connected with the two first words in v. 16a; the text is, however, corrupt, see BHK. The rest of v. 16 makes the second bicolon of the stanza.

56:6—8, are wrongly printed in BHK; the verse division of TM is correct. But TM's interpunction in v. 7 is incorrect; put Athnach to *'aqebåy*. Read in v. 6 *yedabberu*, in v. 7 *ba'ᵃšuray* for *ka'ᵃšær*, and *palles* in v. 8.

59:5a is the parallel colon to v. 4b (del. *yhwh*, note the «Elohimpsalter»). Vv. 5b and 6a make the next bicolon; del. '*ælohim* and '*ælohe yiśrå'el*. — As for the three first words in v. 8, see below p. 62.

Wrong division of the lines we have in **62:4**; in connection with the metaphor of people running to overturn a weak wall, *teraççehu* of course is impossible, read *tåruçuhu* and transfer *keqir nåṭuy* behind '*iš*. Then we get 2 perfect Qinah stichoi, as the other «long verses» in the psalm.

The verse division in **64:6—7** is incorrect; a concurrent cause has been the absurdity of the corrupted text in v. 7: «they search out (or: dig for) wickedness (or: burnt sacrifices); we are whole, a search is searched out, the inward of a man and a deep heart». In v. 6c the words of the wicked are quoted, they imagine that nobody can see them, scil. their evil deeds; according to the rule of duality and thought rhyme, we except a second colon, continuing their words; it then seems very probable that the verb *ḥpś* in some or other way speaks about the supposed inscrutinability of their secret plans. BHK proposes ingeniously to read in direct continuation of v. 6c: *weyahpoś taʿlumotenu:* «who can see us and find out our secret plans?» Then the next bicolon v. 7b begins with *hefæś.* As it logically must have had some nearer connection also with v. 8 — cpr. impf. cons. *wayyorem* — it seems very probable that it was a statement about the wicked enemies, not a continued quotation of their words. In the letters *hpś mhpś* we then probably have to see a verb and a noun (nomen actionis) of the stem *hpś.* I propose: *hithappeśu mhpś* (pronunciation uncertain), and *'ånuś* (BHK, Jer. 17:9): «they make themselves a thing that needs to be searched out», i.e. they make themselves unknowable, (their) inward deceitful and (their) heart deep» — but God shall shoot them, etc. — However one may judge about the details of this emendation, so much seems quite certain, that in vv. 6—7 we have to do with 3 bicola, not with 2 tricola.

The case is much easier in vv. *9—10.* Here, too, TM divides the verses incorrectly; v. 10a is the parallel colon to v. 9b, as shown by BHK. In v. 9a read *wayyaślik yhwh ʿålemo,* as he cannot very well let «their tongue» fall upon them, but the evil words of their tongue; at least a *dibre* has fallen out, and perhaps, also an adjective «evil» or the like.

In BHK **66:1b—7** are printed as if these verse were tricola. In fact they are not. The whole psalm is written in regular bicolic Mashal metre, 2 and 2 bicola making a stanza. V. 2a must be connected with v. 2b, giving the theme of the song of praise v. 2b and thus rounding off the 1st stanza. Then a verb ovbiously is lacking before *berob,* e.g. *'attå mośel,* cpr. v. 7. Vv. 3b, c, 4a, b make the 2nd stanza. The 3rd: vv. 5a, b, 6a, b; the 4th vv. 6c, 7a—c.

In **69:14—15** the division in TM is right, the print of the lines in BHK wrong. But v. 14 consists of two bicola; read *tihyæ ʿet råçon,* put Athnach to *råçon.* TM's division i vv. **15—17,** however, is wrong, put Soph pasuq after *miśśoneʾåy.* The two last words in v. 15 must be connected with v. 16, but a verb, e.g. *naśśeʾeni,* must be supplemented. Athnach to *mayim,* new bicolon with *weʾal tiblåʿeni,* as in BHK. — In vv. **20—21,** too, the verse division is wrong; *kol-çoreray* must be connected with v. 21: «Oh, all my enemies!»

In **71:18** the last word must be connected with v. 19, which thus becomes two complete bicola, the second beginning with *'ašær*.

75:2 seems in the interpunction of TM to be a tricolon, although an extremely bad one. The consonantal text represented by G, shows the correct division of this bicolon. G is, however, wrong in its vocalization of the text. Read *weqore'e bešimekå sipperu* (BHK).

In **90:4** the two last words *we'ašmurå ballaylå* must be connected with v. 5a; «a watch in the night» feels very long and would be a very bad metaphor for the shortness of the life in parallelism with *'ætmol*. Now *zåramtåm* v. 5 is absolutely senseless; when connecting *'weašmurå ballaylå* with v. 5, however, it becomes quite clear how to emend: *zimmantåm* (or *zimmantå låmo*): «a watch in the night thou givest them as their appointed time». The parallel colon must be found in v. 5b, where, however, the original text has been confused by doublets from v. 6a, as seen in all newer commentaries. Now Job 14:14, where man's life is seen as a watch, shows that *hålaf* is used about the relief from the watch; as original text in v. b we may suppose: *yahᵉ lefu, šenå yihyu:* «then they are relieved and fall asleep». *babboqær kehåçir* in fact belongs to v. 6, where *babboqår* and *wehalaf* are dittographies; read *babboqær kehaçir yåçiç, lå'æræb* etc. — On the intention and composition of Ps. 90, see below pp. 50ff; on v. 17 below p. 65.

The verse division in **95:7** is undoubtedly wrong; v. 7b begins a quite new thought and liturgical scene, and introduces vv. 8ff. See below pp. 66.

To **102:27b** v. 28(a) is the antithetic parallel colon.

104:25 is incorrectly divided in BHK; v. b and c are the parallel cola of a thought rhyme and make a bicolon, and had thus to be printed on the same line. — V. 25a is a «long verse», a stichos (not a hemistich) itself, but a little too short; see below p. 83.

The first three bicola of **109:1—4** are incorrectly divided in TM, see BHK. Correct division: vv. 1b + 2a (÷ *ufi mirmå*); vv. 2b + 3a; vv. 3b + 4 (÷ *tahat 'ahabåti*, dittography from v. 5, see BHK); read *we'en tiflå* instead of *'wa'ani tefillå*.

130:2a belongs to v. 1: the next Qinah verse runs from *tihyænå*. As for the rest of the psalm, see below p. 54.

In **135:6—7** both the massoretic verse division and the division of the lines in BHK are incorrect. Vv. 6c and 7a must be connected with each other, even if they make no real thought rhyme; vv. 7b,c make the next bicolon. The psalm is clearly built up of regular stanzas, 4 Mashal bicola to the stanza. — On vv. 9 and 11, see below p. 54.

Incorrect is also the verse division in **140:9—10**. This is, however, due to an incorrect text. Read with G (and Ketib) *zåmemu ʿålay;* 9b is a compound nominal clause, the object of which is the clause *zåmemu ʿålay:* «what they are planning against me, grant it not». The first 2 words in v. 10 have no syntactical connexion, a verb is missing; this is found in *yårumu* v. 9; read *ʾal yårimu* (cpr. G and BHK), to be connected with v. 10; *sælåh* must be replaced after *tappeq* v. 9. — In v. 11 read *yamṭer* and *wåʾeš*, with Athnach (BHK). In v. 12 *råʿ* probably is a variant of *ḥåmås*.

143. The metre is Qinah (v. 7a read *ki kåletå*, with 2 Mnss., G; v. 9 + *ki*, G). The division of the verses, and of the printed lines in BHK, is incorrect in as far as vv. **1—3** consist of two Qinah verses each. (In v. 1b a *haqšibå* or the like must be supplemented before *bæʾᵃmunåtækå*). In vv. **11—12**, too, the massoretic division is wrong. The verses build in fact 3 Qinah bicola («stichoi»); Athnach to *beçidqåtækå;* new line with *toçiʾ;* v. 12a is the antithetic parallel to v. 11b; the last Qinah begins with *wěhaʾᵃbådtå*. –As for v. 5c see below p. 71.

More difficult is the question of the correct division of the verses in **Ps 31**. BHK³ connects v. 3a with 2c, but TM is right in taking v. 3a and b as the parallel links of a thought element; correctly a Soph pasuk should have been put after 3b. V. 2 then seems to be a tricolon; but G and the parallel 71:2 here add a *wehaççileni;* accordingly, something has been lost in TM, the rest of which is found in the G text, and we may conclude that v. 2 originally has included 2 Qinah stichs (bicola). — As v. 4a cannot be connected with v. 3c,d (see above), the division of the lines in BHK³ here is wrong. But v. 4 is obviously much too long for a

Qinah, and even for a Mashal bicolon, without, however, making any real tricolon. One Hebr. Mns and S have *yhwh* after *šiměkå*, and that makes v. 4b a regular Qinah. We are thus entitled to believe that v. 4a, too, originally has been one; the shorter half of the bicolon has been lost. — TM's division of v. 5 is correct; the print in BHK³ is a mistake. — V. 6a begins a new Qinah, which, however, ends with *yhwh*. The 2 last words *'el 'æmæt* must be connected with v. 7a — see the correspondence between *'æmæt* and *šåw* —; read *śn'thšmrym* = *śåne'tå šomerim*. V. 7b begins a new thought element: But I, opposite those who worship the *hable šåw*, trust in Yahweh; consequently, says the parallel membrum v. 8a, I shall (always) have the opportunity of praising Him for his *hæsæd;* what this *hæsæd* actually means, is said in the next two Qinoth v. 8c,d and v. 9: Yahweh has always considered and will always «consider his trouble» and save him from the hand of his enemy. — V. 10 seems to be a tricolon, BHK⁰ proposes to delete the 2 last words *nafši ubiṭni*, but metrically v. 10b (from *'åšešå* incl.) is a correct Qinah. If the psalm has been written in the regular Qinah metre, it is more likely that some words — the shorter half of a Qinah — have been lost after v. 10a. In my opinion the text in v. 10—12 has suffered a little disarrangement, and the words missing in v. 10a are still to be found in the text. It is obvious that *upahad limeyuddå'ay* cannot be separated from the parallel *hærpå liš'kenay* (del. *wě*), as now in BHK³; but then the first part of v. 12 is much too long, the second too short. I propose to transplace the 2 last words in v. 11b *wa'ªçåmay 'åšešu* after *çar-li* v. 10a, and connect the 2 first words in v. 12 *mikkol-çorěråy* with *kåšal be'onyi* (leg. with Σ, BHK³). A new Qinah then begins with *håyiti* v. 12; obviously *upahad limeyuddå'åy* is the shorter parallel membrum of this Qinah; then again a new Qinah from *ro'ay* on; this is, however, too short; we expect a verb even in its first part, and this can be found in the now quite unnecsessary and badly placed *me'od*, emended in *ma'ªsuni*. — Vv. 18—19 belong logically together; v. 19 might be taken as a tricolon, whereas v. 18 looks like a 4 + 4 bicolon. V. 19b is, however, a regular Qinah, and, seen from the viewpoint of the Qinah metre, vv. 18a (÷ *yhwh*) and 19a, represents a longer colon, vv. 18b and 18c a shorter colon respectively. Now logically v. 18c *yiddemu liš'°ol* belongs after v.

19a: let the wicked be ashamed, scil. through the failure of their evil plans (18b), let these lying lips be put to silence (19a), yea may they be silent in She'ol. No doubt this is the right order. By placing v. 18c after v. 19a, we get 2 regular Qinah bicola.

With these emendations the psalm appears as though built up of 12 stanzas, 3 Qinah verses to each stanza; the only exception are vv. 20—21 with 4 Qinah verses. On v. 24 see p. 77.

To this group: wrong division of the verses, belongs even **1 Sam. 2:9—10**. The parallelism clearly shows that v. 10d,e are the two membra of a bicolon; the same is obviously the case with vv. 10b and c; read in b *'ælyon* (BHK) ⧧ *yhwh*. Parallel cola of the same bicolon are in fact also vv. 9c and 10a (read *yåḥeṭ meribåw*).

If the text in **Jonah 2:6—7** is at least roughly correct, the verse division must be wrong. This thanksgiving psalm is written in Qinah verses, and then the 2 first words in v. 7 must be connected with v. 6 and corrected as proposed in BHK. But in all probability the damage goes deeper.[1]

4.

Now we have to deal with apparent tricola in TM where *other text witnesses, Hebrew mss., G and/or some other old version, have a longer and obviously better text*, that demonstrates that the tricolon in question originally has been 2 bicola. The proof of the superiority of the longer text is in the first line the exegetical considerations, the demands of context and logic. When the longer text even gives the psalm in question a regular metrical structure, we get strong corroboration of the correctness of the text-critical

---

[1] *hå'åræç* v. 7, here = the nether word, has no syntactical connection; in v. c a predicate is missing; some words must have been lost. Add *'æl taḥtiyyot* before *hå'åræç*, and a *nisgeru* after this word; *le'olåm* contradicts the following narrative about the salvation; originally the text may have had a parallel membrum after *ba'aday*, e.g. *weša'aræhå ni'ålu* (niph.perf. *n'l*). Then the short membrum is missing behind v. 6c. The narrative about the salvation begins very abruptly in v. 7a; I suggest that a Qinah like this: *we'attå šålahtå yådekå/wattiqqaheni mibbor* has fallen out before v. 7c; cpr. 18:15; 40:3.

and exegetical argument; we may even feel sure that the better text is the author's text.

13:6 is no real tricolon with a more or less strong parallelism; v. 6e begins a new thought element and makes now an isolated single colon. But G has the missing parallel colon: *wa'ªzammerå šem yahwh ʿælyon,* cpr. 7:18.

62:9. This psalm is a national «psalm of protection» (see Birke-land, *The Evildoers in the Book of Psalms,* pp. 28f) in public danger; the praying one, the worshipper, is the representative of the people, probably the King. The metre is Qinah. Even in v. 4, from the mere formal point of view we have 2 Qinoth, curiously enough in BHK printed on 1 line; but the parallelism is here rather a queer one: first the two parallel verbs; then the two parallel comparisons; obviously *kĕqir nåṭuy* must be replaced after *'iš,* read in 4b

> *ʿåd 'ånå tehótetú | ʿal 'iš kĕqir nåṭúy*
> *tåruçúhu kúllĕkæm | gådér haddéḥuyå.*

In v. 5 read *lehašš'oto* for *miśśe'to.*

Among these regular Qinoth we now meet three apparent tri-cola: vv. 9, 12 and 13. Here we have to deal with *v. 9.* The second part of the verse from *šifku* incl. forms a regular Qinah. The first part is too short for a Qinah, but too long to form only the first longer colon of a Qinah. Now G instead of *bekol ʿet* has *kol ʿådat,* pre-ferred by BHK and many commentators. Apparently rightly; for in TM the following word *ʿåm* has no logical and syntactical con-nection with the preceding words. But the metrical irregularity remains. The solution is, that both texts, TM and G, are necessary. In v. 9 the worshipper faces his compatriots, the whole congregation of the people (G) and asks them to trust Yahweh, as he himself does, but the tenor and the tune of the psalm demand that he expressly says: not only in the actual danger, but at all times (TM). Accordingly, the original text had both «the whole congregation of the people» and the «at all times»:

> *biṭhu bo bĕkol ʿet | kol ʿådat ʿåm.*

The graphic similarity of the two expressions closely besides each other, makes it easy to understand that one of them was lost. The G text has lost *bekol ʿet,* the TM type has lost *kol ʿadat.*

The G text allows us, by combination of the two text types, to restore two regular Qinah verses. — On vv. 12—13 see below p. 79.

67:5 is in Albright's opinion (*op.cit.* p. 6) «a tricolon according to the scheme abc/def/chg, with a key word repeated». A glance at the metre of the context suffices to prove that G is right when reading after *tišpoṭ: tebel beçædæq, tišpoṭ;* these words have in TM been lost by homoioteleuton. In the text of G v. 5 gives two perfect Mashal metre bicola, as are all the other «long verses» (stichoi) of the psalm. — V. 8 too, Albright takes as a tricolon, according to the scheme de /gh/ ik. In this metrical interpretation we meet the old Sieversian ghost «den Sechser» (2 + 2 + 2). In fact v. 8 is, as are all Sievers's «Sechser», a Mashal 4 + 4 bicolon:

yebárekénu 'ælohím | wĕyir'ú 'otó kol-'áfse[1] 'árç.

73:28. G has a plus: *bĕša'ᵃre bat çiyyon*. Styletypological, «form historical» reasons show that the mentioning of the place where the saved worshipper recites his thanksgiving psalm (and tenders his thank offerings) belongs to the typical elements in a thanksgiving psalm — as Ps. 73 undoubtedly is one; cpr. 116:18f. As a rule, the place is, of course, the temple, where the worshipper gives his witness «before the great congregation». In our case, he promises to «tell about God's wonders» on every occasion, whenever he sits together with his fellow men discussing the affairs of the city and telling and hearing news «in the gates of Zion».

In **80:15a** we undoubtedly have to do with an abbreviated writing of the refrain, the full form of which we have in vv. 4, 8, 20.

But the strophic composition of the psalm also shows that the right place of the refrain is not before v. 15(b), but after vv. 15b, 16. The parallel colon to v. 15b is v. 16a; *zot* is here the relative pronoun: the vine which thou hast planted; to *gæfæn zot* is *wekanná* (vok. *kánæ = qánæ*, Hitzig and others) *'ašær* a textual variant. V. 16b is only a doublet to v. 18b; the *bæn 'ádám* is the King, the representative of the people, parall. «the man of thy right hand», and not the vine, as he should be if his right place were in v. 16b.

---

[1] On the retraction of the accent (Sievers: «Tonverschiebung»), rather common in stat. constr., see *ZATW* 68, pp. 119f.

The second shorter colon of the Qinah period **108:2a** = 57:8, which is missing in TM, is found in 5 Hebr. Mss., G, and S, and is undoubtedly correct.

In **147:8** G has a plus *la*ᶜᵃ*bodat hå᾽ådåm*. The whole verse is made after the pattern in 104:14 and must accordingly be filled up with the words *we*ᵉ*eçæb la*ᶜᵃ*bodat hå᾽ådåm*. G has preserved the last two words, and helps us to restore two regular Mashal bicola.

5.

Then there are *cases where an apparent third colon is missing in one or more of the other Hebr. Mss. G, S or other text witnesses,* and where, accordingly, TM has been secondarily enlarged. As a rule, this conclusion can be corroborated by exegetical reasons.

Very simple is the case in **94:23**, by Tsewat taken as a sample of repetitive parallelism. The second *yaçmitem* is missing in some Hebr. Mss. and in G, and then at all events the repetitive parallelism disappears. Moreover, in a real repetitive parallelism the second colon should not only repeat a single word, but also add something to the thought, here, however, follows in TM only a vocative. The second *yaçmitem* is nothing but a simple dittography — note that the two words stand directly beside each other — and the verse is a normal Mashal bicolon (*yhwh* or *᾽ælohim* may be deleted, BHK), as are all the other real «long verses» (stichoi) in the psalm.

Another case is **18:14**, which now seems to be a tricolon; but v.c is missing both in G and in 2 Sam. 22:14 and is certainly to be deleted. — In v. 43a 2 Sam. 22 has a shorter text, which fits the Mashal metre of the psalm much better; the text of v. a in Ps. 18 in fact fits in no Hebrew metrical structure.

Among the isolated tricola Albright also counts **92:10**. But in spite of the very close Ugaritic analogy, quoted by Albright, we cannot neglect the fact, that v. 10a is missing in 3 Hebr. Mss. and in G^B, which obviously means: in the original G; the «colon» is nothing but a dittography of the next clause 10b. Realizing this, we find that the psalm is built up of 5 regular stanzas, 3 bicola in Mashal metre to each stanza — certainly no accident, but consciously planned by the pcet.

In **103:20** the apparent third colon is missing in 1 G Ms. and in S, obviously rightly; the words are quite superfluous. — In a so regularily built up poem we may well believe that also v. 17a has been secondarily expanded; s. BHK.

In **118:15f** Albright finds «a tricolon abc/abd/abc (in which the third colon is identical with the first, a fact which suggests its inorganic relation to the present context) and a normal bicolon abc/abd» (*op.cit.* p. 7). The parenthesis shows that A.s «15f» means v. 15b—16, which in fact build a stanza. This is, however, a quite regular one, consisting of two bicolic «stichoi» in Mashal metre; of such stanzas the whole psalm is built up. The «colon» 16b, which is verbotim identical with v. 15b, is missing in one Hebrew manuscript and in many Greek, and without the slightest doubt rightly. — When one has recognized that Ps. 118 is a processional psalm, in all probability belonging to the New Year festival, there is absolutely no reason to speak of the stanza's «inorganic relation to the present context». — With more right, one could speak of a tricolon in v. 27. This irregularity may be due to the fact that the psalm has a very dramatic character with changing scenes and voices. I am, however, more inclined to suppose that a colon has been lost during the transmission, s. below p. 84.

130:7a is rightly missing in some G Mss.; in the others, the words in all probability are added after «veritas Hebraica». The admonition «May Israel hope in the Lord» is quite out of place between the poet's expression of his confidence vv. 5—6 and the motivation of this confidence in v. 7b,c.

Finally, it may be mentioned that **20:8** is, of course, no real tricolon of a (hypothetical) type $2 + 2 + 4$ (or 5), but a regular Mashal bicolon; delete with G^A *yhwh*, or better *'ælohenu*.

6.

In other cases the apparent tricola obviously are due to textual corruption — or slip of memory in the oral transmission.

Sometimes this is clearly *demonstrated by the alphabetic acrostich* of the psalm in question. The use of such an acrostich presupposes metrical and strophical regularity, as can be seen both in Pss. 111

and 112 and in the alphabetic Lamentations. An acrostich either *is*, or it *is* not. Doubt about the original and intended full regularity of an acrostical poem is absolutely unjustified. A lacuna or an error in an acrostich is of course not the fault of the author, but that of the transmission, oral or textual.

Such textual corruption is certainly to be found in **25:1,5,7**. None of these verses are real tricola, see above pp. 17ff.

V. 1 is incomplete, now consisting of one hemistich («colon») only; the alphabetic scheme, however, shows without doubt that the first word in v. 2 *'ælohay* must be connected with v. 1, otherwise we should have no Beth-distich; this *'ælohim*, however, must originally have had a continuation, which has now been lost. — According to the alphabetic pattern, the Waw-stichos must begin with v. 5b; before the first word we have therefore to put in the text the *wĕ-*, now missing in the TM, but testified by some Hebr. Mss., by G and S. But even so, the «colon» v. 5b is incomplete; it becomes logically and stylistically satisfying if we put v. 7b, which now also breaks the alphabetical scheme, after v. 5b. The psalm thus becomes regularily bicolic, one bicolon for each of the letters of the alphabet.

A similar case we have in **37:20, 25**, where the Daleth-stanza v. 7 is too short and must be filled up from the Chet-stanza v. 14, which is too long; and according to the alphabetich acrostic v. 25c must be replaced after v. 20a. Similarily in vv. *34, 40*; the words *yĕfallĕṭem merĕšá'im* v. 40 have had their original place behind v. 34a. See BHK.

The alphabetic acrostich shows that in **10:4ff**, too the text is corrupted, as agreed by the most mcdern commentators, even if opinions disagree about how to heal it. This point, however, we do not need to discuss here in detail. In TM vv. *5, 8, 9* appear as tricola. But BHK is certainly right in letting the Nun-stanza begin with *ni'eç yhwh*, v. 3, which must then be connected with v. 4; this verse then gets 3 cola; the 3rd begins with *kol-mĕzimmotåw*, a predicate *yigmår* must be supplemented; the 4th colon of the stanza is v. 5a. Instead of *mårom* v. 5b we must read *sårim* (cpr. BHK) as the first word of the Samek-stanza, consisting of vv. 5b, 6.

The Peh-stanza consists of vv. 7a, b, 8a, b. V. 8c, then, is the first colon of the Ayin stanza, comprising also v. 9, with its 3 cola. — Psalms 9/10 are built up of regular stanzas, 2 Mashal bicola to the stanza — as the acrostich testifies.

We have now found some 83 cases where the apparent tricola are only due to false verse division, to displacement of some part of a verse, or to omissions and additions attested by other text witnesses.

7.

Now we shall look at some cases where the question can be settled only by means of *conjecture*.

In this paragraph 7 we shall deal with cases *where more or less evident exegetical reasons show that TM has a corrupted text.*

a) We begin with cases where it is more or less obvious that a *colon (or bicolon) has come in at a wrong place*. This can be due both to mis-rembering in the oral transmission, and to mistakes by the scribe. We have already seen that such is the case in the alphabetic psalms 25 and 37, and 9/10, and, therefore, it might have happened in other cases as well.

Ps. 81 is a liturgy to the festival of Yahweh's epiphany and the renewal of the covenant (the New Year and Enthronement festival), see the Author's *Psalmenstudien* II, 1922, pp. 152ff; *Offersang og Sangoffer*, pp. 156ff. It has a partial parallel in Ps. 95, where the introductory hymn of praise expressly points to the Enthronement of Yahweh. The formula *81:6c*, which introduces the very speech of Yahweh, stands of course outside the metrical scheme; it ought, however, in TM to have been connected with v. 7. — Yahweh's speech, «the oracle» first mentions the benefactions that are the basis itself of the covenant: the exodus and the liberation from the house of bondage vv. 7—8b; then the basic commandment, to worship no other God v. 9—10, for Yahweh is just the God who led the people out of Egypt, v. 11a, b. The presupposition of the renewal of the covenant, however, is that Israel now again, as so often before, has broken the convenant by its sins;

this was seen already during the wandering in the wilderness, as
soon as Yahweh wanted to test Israel through hunger and thirst;
would it then really trust His promises? v. 11c. But Israel failed
the test, and neither trusted Him nor obeyed His commandments,
v. 12, and had to bear the punishment, v. 13. But now, «to day»
(95:7) He again is willing to renew the covenant, «will they now
hearken unto me»? v. 14ff. — It is quite clear that *v. 8c*, which
expressly mentions the place of testing, the waters of Meribah, in
TM comes too early, it belongs together with *v. 11c* (as already
Duhm) and must be replaced before this latter colon; v. 11c is
just the content of the test.

So the latter part of the psalm vv. 7ff appears to consist of
the regular «basic stanzas», two Mashal bicola to the stanza. I think
that this is a good corroboration of our conjecture.

18:44 is apparently a tricolon, as is v. **49** too. Vv. 44a and
49a are rather nearly identical, what long ago has led commentators to propose to transfer v. 49b behind v. 44a, cpr. BHK. But
one will see that v. 49 takes up again a theme that is already
treated in vv. 36—46: how Yahweh gave the worshipper (the King)
strength to win the battle, and saved him in the overwhelming
personal danger in the combat, so that the enemies have now
surrendered and become his slaves. With v. 47 begins the last
section of the psalm, the explicit words of thanks in the usual form
of the benediction: «Yahweh liveth, blessed be my Rock, the God
who giveth me revenge and subdueth nations under me»; this
appositional clause v. 48 in participle form *hannoten* (2 Sam. 22
has the participle *umorid* in v. 48b as well), shortly recapitulates
the content of the picture in vv. 36—46. Here is not the right
place for taking up again details from the battle picture, as does
now v. 49; the right and stylistically correct continuation of the
«blessing» is the renewed words of thanks in v. 50f, introduced by
ʿal-ken. — The consequence of this exegetical consideration is that
v. 49 is a displaced variant of v. 44; the latter has the correct place,
but none of them has the complete text. The right continuation
of v. 44a is v. 49b, c; the parallel colon to 49c is 44b; the next
bicolon consists of 44c and 45a; the too short 46a is nothing but

a doublet to 49b; thus 45b and 46b build the last bicolon of the vv. 44—46.

In this connection I want to deal also with vv. **12** and **31**, the discussion of which systematically belongs to § 7c or 8d. In *v. 12* read *wayyảšæt* (G, T, 2 Sam. 22); *sukkảto* is better placed before *sĕbibotảw*, thus the first bicolon is all right. The rest of the verse is much too long for a single colon, too short, however, for a real bicolon; but a verb is obviously missing; add *mitkassæ be-*, and *weʿảnản* (cpr. Ex. 19:9) at the end; thus the second bicolon is restored. — *V. 31* is also too long for a single colon and must originally have been an ordinary bicolon; add *ûmiśgảb* behind *mảgen*.

Having undertaken the above text-critical operations, we realize, that Ps. 18 is built up of regular stanzas, 4 bicola to each stanza — in my opinion certainly a corroboration of the exegetical-critical result.

22:16—17 are now two apparent tricola. Here we are, however, confronted with the old exegetical crux v. 17c. *kảʾảri yảday wĕraglay,* as it stands is nonsense. If *kảʾảri* is the correct reading, then it is quite clear that some words have fallen out, i.a. the verb, telling *what* the enemies — in v. a, b pictured as wild beasts — do with the worshipper, and what is «like a lion» or makes him like a lion. Among the readings in Mss. and versions, only those which give a verb, convey any meaning. But both *kảʾru* and *kảʾảru*, perf. of *kwr* = «hollow» or of a byform *kảʾar*, are impossible; «hollow» cannot of course mean «pierce», as AV and the ecclesiastical tradition translate; some have tried to give the word the meaning «gnaw», but why should the enemies, imagined as lions and wild oxen (r. in v. 17 *remim* = *rĕʾemim*, as in v. 22), only gnaw the worshipper's hands and feet, and not the rest of his (dead) body? The right interpretation is given by Driver in *Expos. Times* 57, p. 193: a *kảrả* IV = Arab. *kảra* = «bind together». In accordance with Symm. ὡς ζητοῦντες δῆσαι, others have long ago proposed ʾ*ảsĕru*. The exegetical explanation of this «they have bound together my hands and my feet», I have already given in my Norwegian translation of the Psalms 1923, with reference to John 11:44. The enemies treat the worshipper as if he already were a dead man; they have buried him v. 16c, having first bound together his hands and feet, as people used to do with the dead v. 17c, and now they are dividing his property among themselves v. 19. — But then it is quite clear, that the description of their hostile attacks must come *before* the mention of his burial. And that again means that both v. 16c and v. 17c have their right place behind v. 18, where they build a regular bicolon with thought rhyme. V. 17a, b, then, where the enemies are pictured as wild beasts, of course have their original place before v. 13f.

Again the strophical composition of the psalm corroborates the above result. It now becomes apparent that at least the whole first part vv. 2—22 is built up of regular stanzas, three Mashal bicola to the stanza. Such a tristich can and must be reconstructed in vv. 2—3 too; behind *'eli* add *haqšibâ li* (G), *'ælohay*, then with *râḥoq* new bicolon, with which also *'ælohay* v. 3a must be connected; read: *lammâ tirḥaq miššaw'âti.*

We have in **42:9** an apparent tricolon, although only from the viewpoint of the inch scale. In fact, it has no metre at all, it is neither a Maschal nor a Qinah, nor a real tricolon (see above § 2c). Nor does it fit the context; in this part of the psalm the worshipper laments that he is forsaken by God, vv. 7—8, 10—11, whereas v. 9 tells that Yahweh «commands his *ḥæsæḏ* by daytime», scil. to his help. V. 9 at least does not belong where it now stands. This is corroborated by the observation that the refrain 42:6, 12; 43:5 divides the psalm in 3 equally long stanzas — apart from v. 9. — But from where has the verse come in at its present place? Now we observe that 43:2 is nothing but a weaker repetition of 42:10. The question arises, if 42:9 would be a somewhat disarranged form for the original 43:2, added in the margin by another traditionist (scribe). The original form, ot course, should have been 2 full Qinoth, which might be restituted as follows:

> *yomâm çawwê ḥásdekâ | 'elây 'él ḥayyây,*
> *ballâylâ yehi mišórekâ | weçídqâtekâ 'immí.*

On **52:7** see p. 78.

65 is written in Qinah metre. This is evident in the first part of the psalm; quite evident is also that the Massoretic verse division in vv. 2—4 is wrong: the right division has BHK. The 2 Qinah bicola of v. 9 are a little too short; in 9a an *ᵓælohim* (originally *yhwh*) may be supplemented, in 9b an *ᵓattá* at the end. — The theme of the psalm is the thanksgiving of the congregation for the blessings of the year, the fill of crops and cattle, considered from the «mythological» aspect: Yahweh's renewed victory over the primeval demoniac powers and his recreation of the cosmos. In this context the «tumult of the nations» *v. 8* has no place; the verse is too long, but *wahamon leᵓummim* is a gloss with the intention of giving the mythological picture a historical interpretation; the original text has been: *mašbit šᵉᵓon yammim wahámon gallehæm*. — From v. 10c on (*pælæg ᵓælohim* etc.) the metre is unclear, and v. 14 seems now to be a tricolon. But v. 11 consists in fact of 2 bicola (against BHK). V. 13a must no doubt be connected with v. 12 as the parallel second colon to 12b, cpr. *yirᵉáfun ‡ yirᵉáfu*. Vv. 13b and 14 make 2 Qinah bicola; v. 14a and b belong together as parallel cola; 14c is in fact the parallel colon to 13b, cpr. *gilu ‡ yitroᵉáᵉu* and must be replaced before 14a. Vv. 12—13a have only 3 cola instead of the expected 4, v. 10c—e, however, have 3 instead of 2. Then there can be little doubt that v. 10e *ki ken tekinæhá* must be replaced behind 12a.

After this rearrangement we see that the psalm is built up of 5 quite regular stanzas, 4 Qinah bicola to each stanza: vv. 2—4, vv. 5—6, vv. 7—9, vv. 10a—d, 11, vv. 12 (+ 10e)—14. There is every reason to believe that this structure was intended by the author.

68:5,7 now appear as 2 tricola. The present order of the cola, however, cannot be correct. The stanza vv. 5—7 plays on two motifs: a) Yahweh's name, epiphany and abode, b) his saving deeds with the helpless. In TM these two motifs are intermingled. There can, however, be no doubt that vv. 6a and 7b belong together as parallel cola, and that v. 7c is the antithetical parallel to v. 7a. Vv. 6a, 7b must be replaced between vv. 6b and 7a, and the tricola disappear. See the present author's *Der Achtundsechzigste Psalm*, Oslo 1953, pp. 26f.

A rearrangement of the cola must necessarily be undertaken in **68:30—35** as well; see my above-mentioned book. The correct order

of the lines of the two last stanzas — 4 Mashal bicola to the stanza
— is: vv. 29 + *mehekålekå* v. 30, 31a, 31c, 30, 31b, 32; vv. 33, 35a,
34, 35b, 36.

The rearrangement has not been done here on metrical grounds,
but according to the content and the logical sequence and the thought
rhyme rule, i.e. on exegetical and stylistical grounds. Only as a
secondary instance has recourse been made to the metre in special
meaning. But, of course, the metrical results have been taken into
consideration as a corroboration of the exegetical. (This against the
review of A. R. Johnson in the *SOTS Booklist 1955*, p. 35.)

With **86:16** TM rightly lets a new «long verse (stichos)» begin;
after the lament in v. 14 and the expression of the confidence in v.
15, the very prayer for help comes in v. 16. But according to the
parallelism, v. 16b and c belong together as a bicolon. The same
do v. 17b and c, describing the effect of the hoped for help. In fact
vv. 16a and 17a belong together: that Yahweh «turns to him and
shows mercy upon him», may appear in His giving him a «token
for good», a luck-promising oracle. In all probability, v. 16a
must be replaced after 16b,c, making a regular bicolon together
with v. 17a.

In *vv.* **2—3** too, some words have been displaced. V. 2 may
be read as a tricolon; if one believes in the existence of two-beat
cola in Hebrew poetry, we may find a pentacolon. Even the first
colon in v. 3 consists of 2 words (pedes) only. A two-beat unity,
however, does not exist as an independent metrical unity, a «colon»,
only as part of a dipodic 4-beat colon; see above p. 7. Now, however,
the position of the words in v. 2b is impossible; logically the apposition *hab-boṭeaḥ 'elækå* refers only to *'abdekå*, according to its
position, however, it must be connected with *'ælohay*, which is
logically impossible; *'attå 'ælohay* cannot stand where it now stands;
it obviously must be replaced after *'adonåy* v. 3, see BHK. Thus
vv. 2—3 make two regular Mashal bicola.

Even another displacement seems to have happened to this
psalm. The transition from v. 13 to v. 14 seems rather abrupt;
we expect a new introduction to the renewed lament and description
of the hostilities of the enemies v. 14ff. If we replace v. 7, at least

unnecessary in its present place, before v. 14, we shall find that the psalm is built up of 6 regular stanzas, 3 Mashal bicola to the stanza — scarcely an accident only. On v. 14 see below § 8b, p. 74.

Most commentators agree that the original order of the stichoi in **87** has been disarranged; cpr. the proposed order in BHK[3]. With *yesudâto* the psalm cannot have begun; the suffix hangs in the air, without reference. The psalm is a «Zion hymn», an indirect hymn of praise on Yahweh through the praise of his holy city, which he has founded, elected and glorified. The only verse of the preserved text, that suits as the starting line, is v. 2, a Qinah bicolon. As not seldom, the hymn of praise starts with a general statement of the praiseworthiness, not with a call to praise. The first definite thing to be said of Zion, is her foundation by Yahweh himself; accordingly v. 1b must follow v. 2. Now v. 1b is only the first (longer) half of a Qinah; the parallel membrum, however, is obviously v. 5c, making the second (shorter) half of the Qinah. Thereupon follows logically the third Qinah v. 3, expressing the special religious quality of Zion: it has got the name «City of God» (originally: Yahweh); in TM these words are taken as a vocative: «O, city of God», but *medubbâr* indicates that the verse speaks of the name, given to Zion; so we must supplement a *tiqqâre'* in v. 3b, thus making the Qinah complete.

Vv. 4—6 give a new picture: Yahweh «counting (or: writing?) in the book of the nations» (r. *bik'tab*, see BHK[3]) and mentioning the different peoples in their relation to Zion. The logic of the description of the picture demands, however, that v. 6 shall be placed before vv. 4—5. Obviously v. 4c corresponds to v. 6b; together the two *zæ yullâd šâm* make the second half of the fifth Qinah 6 + 4c. Then follows quite logically v. 4a, b, the sixth Qinah, mentioning in opposition to all the other nations Zion, «the mother» of them all; the text presupposed by G: *'em 'omer* (or: *ye'âmer*), and then: *'iš wâ'iš* is obviously correct; the *û-* before *lĕçiyyon* is adversative: «But of Zion He says: Mother, every one is born in her».

The two sections of the psalm, so far discussed, consist of 3 Qinah verses each.

V. 7 introduces a new picture, an impression from the cultic
festivals of Zion, characterized by their «singing and dancing». But
the text is obviously fragmentary; at least a verb is missing, telling
what the singers and dancers are doing. We may, perhaps, supplement a *yodukå* or the like. This single, seventh, Qinah, however,
is too meagre for a poetical picture of the cultic relevance of Zion.
Like the verb in v. 7, the last part of the poem has also been lost;
the psalm is only a fragment. Remembering the even balance of
the two first «stanzas»: 3 Qinoth to each, we are entitled to say that
at least 2 Qinoth have been lost.

The psalm thus gives no evidence of tricola or isolated single
cola.

In **91** we find two apparent tricola, *vv.* **4** *and* **7**. V. 4, however,
is no real tricolon (see above § 2c); the metaphor «shield and
buckler» 4c does not suit the metaphor of Yahweh as the mother
bird who «covers» the pious «with her feathers and under her wings»,
4a,b. On the other hand, v. 7c, the main clause following the
concessive clause v. 7a,b, is very abrupt and indefinite. There can
be little doubt that v. 4c had its original place after v. 7c (BHK);
thus both the apparent tricola disappear. — The result is corroborated by the observation that we thus get 4 regular stanzas, 4
Mashal bicola to the stanza. That the first lines of the psalm are
lost, most modern critics agree.

102:27 is an apparent tricolon, whereas v. 28 consists of a
single colon only. The matter is, however, not so simple as it seems
in BHK, where vv. 27c and 28 are printed on the same line as the
parallel cola of a bicolon. — But first we have to look a little at
v. 24ff. Here begins a new thought, compared with the preceding
verses. In contradiction to the confidence, based on earlier experiences, expressed in vv. 13—23, the worshipper in v. 24 states
that Yahweh has forsaken him, «weakened his strength in the way
and shortened his days». Here we expect to find the subject, Yahweh,
expressly mentioned; in v. b, too, a word or two seems to have
been lost. At all events, *'omar 'eli* cannot be separated from v. 25
and connected with v. 24, as BHK does, adhering to G, S; v. 25
expresses the consequence of v. 24: because Yahweh has forsaken

him, «therefore I now say» — a new element in the sequence of
the thoughts. But here an *'åni* before *'omer* is absolutely necessary;
this word has fallen out together with the last words of v. 24. Also
a *yhwh* may be supplemented before *'eli*. At all events v. 25 a—b will
do for a complete bicolon. Then, however, v. 25 appears as a tricolon.
But no real one; even v. 25c *bĕdor* etc. is a new thought element
and ought according to the rules of Hebrew poetry begin a new
«stichos» (bicolon). Now, however, it stands without partner. But
v. 28 repeats the same thought, partly with the same words as v.
25c (*šenotækå*). On the other hand, the thought in v. 28 seems
necessary in connection with v. 27. The thought expressed in v. 27
is: they perish and change, thou endurest and art always the same.
This idea is repeated and varied in two bicola:

> [27]they vanish, but thou endurest
>   they all wear out like a robe,
>   thou changest them like garments (and they change),
>   [28a]but thou art still the same . . . .

The solution is obviously to replace v. 28b behind v. 25a,b
and read *yåmækå* for *šenotækå* in v. 25c, and then to supplement v.
28a with an synonymous expression, and read e.g. *wĕ'attå hu'*
le'olåm wǎ'åd. The compound nominal clause vv. 28b, 25c will then
have to be translated as a relative clause:

> thou whose years never end
>   whose 'days' are throughout all generations.

144:7 *can* at least be taken as a tricolon, as it is e.g. by E.
König. With our perception of the nature of the Hebrew verse it
is impossible to rank v. 7b among any known scheme of the colon.
By another inter-punctuation there seems materially to be stuff
enough for 2 bicola. The critical problem is, however, more complicated. V. 7 must be considered in connection with v. 8, a relative
clause (*'ašær*) to v. 7. Now v. 8 is verbotim = v. 11b,c, v. 11a is
found in v. 7, too, partly in v. a, partly in v. b. As the composition
of the psalm gives no ground to take vv. 8, 11 as some sort of
refrain (as König tries to do), it is clear that v. 11 is a textual
doublet to (v. 7 and) v. 8. According to the rules of the «species»
(«Gattung») national psalm of lamentation, spoken by the King

vv. 9ff, the promise of praise correctly makes the last section of the psalm; the promise follows the lament and the prayer.[1] Then v. 11, of course, is out of place where it now stands. Vv. (7—)8 are in the right place within the scheme of the psalm; v. 11 is a displaced variant. — But v. 11 has the better text. To this v. 11, according to all elementary metrical rules, even the two last words in v. 10 must be counted, as G rightly has it; cpr. BHK; put Soph pasuq behind *'abdo*. This restituted v. 11 must replace v. 8.

BHK and many commentators now think that v. 7 must be reconstructed after v. 11a. But then vv. 7(—8),11 should make 3 bicola only; we see, however, that the other bicola in this psalm belong together 2 and 2 (vv. 1 [see below]; 2; 3—4; 5—6; 9—10). We therefore at least ask if vv. 7—8, 11 should not originally have had 4 bicola. And really there seems to be a logical and stylistic gap between *mimmayim rabbim* and *miyyad bene nekâr*. Now v. 7 is clearly a variation of 18:17f (45f). The solution of the critical problem, then, in all probability is this: In the TM tradition v. 11 in its original place as v. 8 has been mis-written (or misremembered) and partly mixed with v. 7, which accordingly, has been mutilated as well; the writer or some later copyist has seen that v. (7—)8 was out of order and therefore put the more correct form of the verse(s) at the margin or between the lines, from where it has come into the text as v. 11. V. 7 must be reconstructed after its model 18:17f. Read:

> [7]*šelâḥ yâdékâ mímmârόm,*
>   *hamšêni mimmáyim rabbim,*
>   *peçéni me'óyebây 'âz*
>   *miśśóne'áy 'âmeçú mimmǽnni,*
> [8(=11)] *'ašǽr pihǽm etc.*

Thus reconstructed vv. 7—8(11) give 4 regular bicola, logically connected 2 and 2.

The psalm consists of regular Mashal bicola, as said above. There seems to be at least one exception, v. 1. I can scarcely think this original. As commentators always have seen, 144 in many respects is an imitation of 18. The model of *v. 1* is 18:47. I do not find it too daring to supplement: *weyârum 'ælohe yišʿi.* — Systematically this case belongs to § 8d.

[1] See *Offersang og Sangoffer*, pp. 227ff, and especially pp. 231f, 235ff.

If vv. 12ff belong to the same psalm — which may be doubted — then they must be taken as a part of an older psalm, which the poet has taken up and very superficially incorporated in his own poem. The verses, then, at all events are a fragment. For this reason we have no certainty that *v.* **14** ever should have made a real tricolon. The surrounding verses make us expect that v. 14a once had a parallel and was a full bicolon; realizing that even in this part of the psalm 2 and 2 bicola respectively have a closer connection to each other, I am inclined to think that $1\frac{1}{2}$ bicolon (3 cola), have been lost in v. 14; cpr. below § 7c.

b) Now we shall deal with such *cases where the exegetical reasons seem to show that secondary elements have intruded in TM and give the false impression of tricola — or of isolated cola amidst regular bicola.* Such secondary elements may be simple dittographies, or textvariants included by some copyist, originally perhaps as marginal notes, or explanatory glosses, originally from the margin.

In **Ps. 2** the introductory remark to the oracle itself, v. 7a, of course, stands outside the metrical structure. The same does v. 12c; this sentence does not belong to the very corpus of the psalm, but is a liturgical refrain; perhaps it is due to the later interpretation and use of the psalm, to which Yahweh, not as originally meant the anointed King, was in the centre of the psalm and the interest of the congregation; see below § 9 p. 88f.

The apparent 3rd colon in *v.* **3** *ʿal yhwh weʿal mešiḥo* is at least a bad verse, since the two *ʿal* must be accentuated to fit in the regular 4 beat scheme. The content of v. 3c is quite correct. But the whole remark is absolutely unnecessary; every hearer (and reader), and especially in the cultic situation of the psalm, knows immediately that the rebellion of the nations and their princes is directed against the King on Zion and his God Yahweh. Thus the suspicion is very likely that v. 3c is no original part of the psalm, but an exegetical remark, and, perhaps, from the above-mentioned later understanding of the psalm, this means an eschatological interpretation of it.

No one can escape seeing that of the bicola of this psalm, 3 and 3 materially and logically hang together and build «stanzas»:

vv. 1—3; 4—6; 7—9; 10—12. I take it for granted that the 2 first words of v. 12 belong to v. 11b, and that Bertholet is right in his conjecture: *naššequ beraglåw bir'ådå*, and that v. 12c does not belong to the psalm-text proper, s. above. — This observation corroborates the above suggestions.

18:51c might, together vith v. a, b, be a real tricolon. The psalm is a casual thanksgiving psalm of a king having experienced Yahweh's miraculous help in battle. Through this salvation Yahweh has demonstrated, as says the last bicolon of the last stanza, that ‹he gives his King great victories and shows loving kindness to his anointed», i.e. the worshipping definite historical King himself. To this confession v. 51c «to David and his seed for evermore» obviously is a generalizing explanatory addition — true in itself according to Israelite faith, but not fitting into *this* context. It may have been added as the psalm was later used on other similar occasions.

At the first glance **38:13** might give the impression of a tricolon, s. the 3 verbs *wayenaqqešu — dibberu — yæhgu*. But just as v. 12 has been expanded by doublets (*ya'ᵃmodu — 'åmådu*), so the same seems to be the case in v. 13 (*wynqšw — mbqšy;* s.i.a. Delitzsch, Baethgen). Now vv. 12—13 make a stanza; accordingly there must be a closer connection between these 2 verses as to the content; in other words, one expects on the basis of the context that the subject in the two verses must be the same person: as v. 12 says, «my friends and my kinsmen». It thus seems very probable that Gunkel is right in considering *mebaqqeše nafši wedoreše rå'ati* as a gloss, due to some writer's or reader's or oral transmitter's misunderstanding of the verse. Then v. 13 is a regular Mashal bicolon as are all the other «long verses» (stichoi) of the psalm.

46 is, like 42/43, divided by the refrain in 3 equally long, regularly built stanzas; it is certainly only by the scribe's mistake that the refrain is missing after v. 4. The metre is clear cut 4 + 4 Mashal. Only *v.* **10** consists of 3 cola. Syntactically the participle *mašbit* continues the relative clause *'ašær-šåm* etc. v. 9b. Regularly we should expect the inversed order: participle continued by finite verb — let alone the fact that the relative pronoun is prosaic, not poetic style. Moreover, v. 9a does not read as a real 4 beat colon; it consists of 3 pedes only. — All these considerations make it more than probable that v. 9b is a prose gloss; the parallel colon to v. 9a is v. 10a.

In **50:1** the lines are wrongly divided in BHK. The verse builds no real tricolon, *wayyiqrâ' hâ'âræç* as a second colon would be much too short as compared with v. a. This latter is, however, much too long for a normal colon. V. 1 is an introductory formula, advertising the following «speech of reproach». There is no reason, neither logical nor emotional, to stress the introduction of the speaker such as TM now does. *'el* and *'ælohim* are simply variants, and as the psalm is transmitted within the «Elohim-psalter», both of them are «corrections» of the original *yhwh* which also has been preserved in TM. Then v. 1a and b are the two parallel cola of a regular Mashal bicolon. The parallel bicolon is *v. 2*; b is, however, a little too short; the original text may have had *yhwh 'ælohenu*; a 1. pers. plur. suffix, stressing the close relations between the *theos epiphanes* and the people and thus also the responsibility of the latter, is here, in fact, wanted. The description of the epiphany follows in v. 3b, 4ff. On v. 3a see below p. 73, on v. 7 p. 61.

The verse lines in **57:8—9** are wrongly divided in BHK; the verse division af TM is correct. But the two verses only apparently are two tricola. In v. 8, *nåkon libbi* rightly is missing in the doublet 108:2, and then v. 8 is an ordinary bicolon. The same is, in fact, v. 9 too; instead of *kebodi* 1 Hebr. Ms. and S have *kinnori*, which is obviously the correct text: v. 8, the awakening of the person himself, *libbi*, v. **9**, the awakening of the instruments. Then *(we)-kinnor[i]* is the now displaced correction of the miswritten *kebodi*.

75:9c—d is both too short and too long. If, with G and S we read the grammatically correct *miz-zæ 'æl-zæ*, the 3 last words *kol-riš'e hâ'âræç* fall outside a normal bicolon. If this means the evil-doers within the «land» of Israel, the words are a false gloss; the enemies in this «psalm of protection», the *holelim* and *rešâ'im* v. 5 are doubtless the heathen powers. But *'âræç* may as well mean the world. But even then, the said words are quite unnecessary; every hearer and reader should at once understand who were meant. And as an interpretation they only weaken the grand picture in v. 9. They are thus in all probability a secondary gloss.

In **82:5** either v. b, the words *bahašekå yithallåku*, or v. c, *yimmotu* etc. are secondary, if otherwise the Qinah metre is the consequent metre of this psalm. The subject in v. a is the other gods v. 1 whose unjust rule is due to their lack of wisdom, of (moral) understanding; as now the stability of the whole cosmos depends on the «justice» (*çedåqå*) and the wisdom of God, (cp. Job!), or the gods the result of their lack of wisdom is that «all the pillars of the world (*'æræç*) totter». And therefore Yahweh must now take over the rule himself. In this mythological conception the words «they wander in darkness» do not say what necessarily must be said in this connection and what is said in v.c. To wander in darkness mostly denotes disaster; but in Prov. 2:13 and Qoh. 2:14 the expression is used about lack of wisdom. In Ps. 82:5 the said words obviously are a secondary gloss, and probably presuppose the wrong interpretation of «the gods» as human beings.

90:3 is in TM a tricolon in Mashal metre (4-beat cola). Suspicion arises about v. 1, which must be scanned as a Qinah bicolon, the second colon having 3 beats (pedes) only. Moreover, v. 2c is no correct 4 beat colon, but must be read with 6 beats: *umé'olåm we'åd 'olåm 'attå 'él*. Perhaps a displacement of some words has taken place? From the viewpoint of our philosophical logic, we should expect the poet to begin with God's «eternity» (v. 2) and then to speak of his relation to Israel (*lånu* v. 1). On the other hand, we may admit that the poet's logic might be different from ours. In this psalm of lamentation on behalf of the congregation, Israel, the poet then might well take his piont of departure in Yahweh's gracious protection of Israel throughout the generations, from the birth of the nation, unto this day. That would, to the poet, just be the proof that Yahweh has been «the God» from the very beginning, «before the mountains were born, before earth and land were in travail».[1]

---

[1] Curiously enough, most translators and commentators treat *teholel* as a passive or alter the vocalization to *teholal*. TM is quite right: the earth has given birth to the mountains. We have here a reminiscence of the old

But should this way of thinking be in due accordance with the composition of this psalm and the ideas the poet really wants to express? The psalm is a «congregational psalm of lamentation.»[1] The situation, the background of the psalm, is the long-lasting oppression by a foreign power, the permanent situation of the Jewish congregation in post-exilic times. The cultic situation is one of the annual penitential days. During all these years the members of the congregation have been «consumed by God's anger and troubled by his wrath» (v. 7, cp. v. 11) because of their sins (v. 8); the «strength of their days», as the poet ironically says, «has been labour and sorrow, for it was soon cut off, and we flew away» (v. 10b); they have not been able to enjoy «the work of their hands»; the poet obviously means: the fruit of their work has been taken away by foreign oppressors, tax collectors etc. This means nearly the opposite of what is said in v. 1; they have for many years *not* experienced what they, as Yahweh's *hasidim*, felt entitled to expect. The actual point of the psalm is the congregation's prayer for deliverance and restitution vv. 13ff. And in a rather individualizing way, that should be absolutely impossible in the days of Moses, the prayer is motivated by the reference to the short life of individual man (v. 9, 10b): «shall our whole short life be spent in this miserable way?!» «How long?» «Grant us joy as long as thou hast been afflicting us, for all years we have had suffering» (Moffatt). — Against the background of this actual situation and intention the poet's consideration of God's eternity must be seen. It is not his intention to sing a song of praise on God's eternity so to say per se, nor to meditate over this theme. He wants to stress his main motivation of the prayer («Gebetserhörungs-motiv»), the shortness of man's life, by setting it up against God's eternity: willt thou, Eternal God, in whose eyes a thousand years are as one day, and man's short life less than a second of time,

conception of «Mother Earth». See the author's paper «Moder Jord i det Gamle Testament» in *Religionshistoriska studier tillägnade Edvard Lehmann*, Lund 1927, pp. 131ff, and cp. also G. Ricciotti, «E nudo tornerò cola (Giobbe 1,21)», in *Atti dell VIII Congresso internazionale di Storia delle religioni*, Firenze 1956, pp. 274ff.

  [1] See Mowinckel: *Offersang og Sangoffer*, ch. VI, and especially pp. 222ff.

really let even the rest of our short lives pass in sorrow and trouble, as they have done as far?! We confess our sins, but be gracious, Gcd, and have mercy, that we may rejoice again, and establish thou the work of our hands!

Another poet might perhaps have begun with the prayer and the lament, then given the motivation: the shortness and trouble-someness of life, and finally, have stressed this thought by pointing to its opposite, God's eternity. Stylistic tradition and convention, however, demanded that the hymnical part of the composition should form the commencement, cp. 9/10; 27; 40; 89.

I at least feel that v. 1 with its expression of confidence is not the adequate introduction to a psalm built up of these thoughts and composed in this way. Of course, the confidence in Yahweh's *berit* and *hæsæd* is the presupposition, without which the psalm would not have been created. But in the pattern of thought which was in the poet's mind, the expression of this confidence does not fit as an introit. I therefore believe that the metrical irregularity in vv. 1—2 is the result of a later revision of the first stanza, made out of consideration related to that which I have sketched above p. 50. V. 2c is in fact some sort of parallel or variant to v. 1b. Originally v. 1 may have had this wording:

> *yahwǽ me'olǻm 'attǻ hǻyítǻ*
> *umé'olǻm 'attǻ 'él.*

On v. 4 see above p. 28.

There is another verse in this psalm where a secondary addition to the text is found. **90:10a** is neither a real tricolon nor any other metrical verse structure, but only a prosaic gloss. The line breaks the clear logical — and metrical — connection between vv. 9 and 10b: «. . . our years have gone to an end (r. *kǻlu*, S) as a sigh, and their strength (i.e. their content) has been labour and sorrow» (Moffatt: toil, and trouble; the suffix in *rohbǻm* refers to *šǻnenu* v. 9).

On v. 17 see below p. 65f.

An apparent tricolon, although a bad one, we find in **92:12**; according to the Mashal metre of the psalm, v. 12a should be a 4 beat colon, but it has at most 3. In fact the case is very simple:

beqåmim (sic leg. pr. *baqqåmim*) *ʿålay* and *mereʿim* are text variants; of these, the first is the better; only the preposition *be* here gives the verb *šåmaʿ* the meaning demanded by the context: hear triumphant the cry of the fallen enemy. Note also the formal parallelism: *tabbeṭ be-*// *tišmaʿnå be-*.

96:10 is apparently a tricolon, but v. a is a gloss after 98:9. The context of the stanza vv. 10—12 speaks about the reestablishment of the cosmos as the result of Yahweh's enthronization; over this reestablishment the poet calls heaven and earth and ocean and the whole living nature to rejoice. The idea of «judging the nations with justice» has not its right place here, but is the theme of the next stanza v. 13.

That the words *dam benehæm* . . . . . *kenåʿan* in **106:38** is a gloss in prose, I think every modern exeget will agree. Without these words the verse is a correct Mashal bicolon.

115:1 now appears as a tricolon. But it seems quite clear, that when the poet lets the congregation say: «Not unto us, not unto us, but to thy name give glory», i.e. save us not for our sake, but for thy name's sake, then he cannot at the same moment let it say: «for thy mercy's and for thy truth's sake». V. a—b says *expressis verbis* that the congregation hopes for salvation only from God's will to maintain his own glory in the world; v.c appeals to his good feelings and his trustiness against the congregation itself and thus says just the opposite of v. a. There can be no doubt that v. c is a secondary addition, where the glorifying of God's name is interpreted as showing his mercy and trustiness.   ·

115:12 also now appears as a tricolon. But as the context clearly shows, «the house of Israel» here is = «those that fear Yahweh», which again comprises the whole people, «both small and great». It is thus not the intention of the poet to mention the single classes here in vv. 12f. Then v. 12c «He blesses the house of Ahron» is a secondary addition from v. 10. This is the more evident as it is the priests, the house of Ahron, which speak in vv. 12ff and bless the whole congregation.

On **130:1—2** see above p. *29*. The psalm is built up of regular
Qinah verses, two and two making a stanza respectively, *qiwwetå*
v. *5* must be replaced to v. *6a*. On v. *7* see above p. *35*.

In **135:9** *betokeki miçrayim* with its apostrophe of Egypt is
both stylistically and metrically inapporpriate and must be deleted
(BHK). *V.* **11** is logically unnecessary and from the viewpoint of
poetry utterly prosaic. It is no metrical line at all, but a secondary
addition from 136:19f, in the enumerative style of which these
details from the narratives of the Torah are more in place.

137:1—3 seems very irregular from the metrical point òf
view, whether we follow the massoretic interpunction or the printed
lines in BHK. In v. 1, however, the last words *bezokrenu 'æt çiyyon*
even from the exegetical point of view seem quite unnecessary;
it is quite clear from the following lines, that it was the thought
of Zion that was the occasion of the psalm. But not only unnecessary;
the words anticipate in an esthetically dull manner the poem
following. It is just the point of the psalm that it was not the thought
of Zion in general, but the conquerors' requirement of a «Zion song»
that actualized all the sad and bitter feelings and the decision never
to forget Jerusalem. The last words in v. 1 are nothing but a prosaic
commentary of the recitator or the writer. — When they are deleted,
v. 1 comprises a perfect Qinah verse, as are most of the other
verses of the psalm. — But then we expect to find the same metre
also in v. 3. We need only to put *śimhå* behind *śir* and let *wetolelenu*
begin the new bicolon, and we have two regular Qinah bicola in
v. 3.

A secondary element are also the three first words *bat båbæl
haśśedudå* in *v.* **8**. If Babel is already sacked, *haśśedudå*, then a
prayer for her being destroyed should be quite superfluous. The
translation in AV «who art to be destroyed» is a pis-aller that is
philologically unfounded. The same is the proposal to read with
Sym. and BHK *haśśådodå*, if the active form were meant, the better
form would be *śodcdcnu*, cpr. *śobenu* and *tolålenu* v. 3. — If the
hatred of the exulants, their prayer for revenge and the bitter
curse were directed both against Edom and Babel, then it should
be very strange that Babel, the actual destroyer of Jerusalem, «our

tyrants» were mentioned at the second place. It is, however, clear, that Edom, not Babel, is the object of the curse even in vv. 8—9; this is seen from the *hassæla* v. 9, which obviously hints at the Edomite capital Sæla˙! — That Edom, who after the catastrophe in 587 had invaded and occupied the greater part of the old Judean land, still more than Babel was the object of the red-hot hatred of the Jews, is seen from passages as Mal. 1:2f; Isa. 34:5f; 63:1; Ezek. 35:1—15; 36:5; cpr. 32:29; Am. 1:11f; 9:12; Jo. 4:19; Isa 11:14; Jer. 25:21; 49:7—22; Ezek. 25:12—14.

When the text has been corrected in this way, we recognize that the psalm is built up of 3 regular stanzas in a regular Qinah metre, 4 Qinoth to the stanza: vv. 1—3, 4—6, 7—9.

In **139:12** the last words *kahašekå kå᾽orå* (r. *ke᾽orå*) are no third «repetitive» colon; they only say in prose what the bicolon in v. a,b has said in a poetical and correct metrical way. That means that the two words are a gloss. And this gloss is in Aramaic; «light» in Hebr. is *᾽or*, there exists no Hebrew word *᾽orå* = «light» — such a form cannot be concluded from the plur. *᾽orot* Isa. 26:19 — only an *᾽orå* = «luck», «joy», synon. *śimhå* (Esth. 8:16). *hašekå* and *᾽orå* Ps. 139:12 are the Aram. stat. emphat. forms.

Jonah 2:4a is neither a real tricolon nor a Sieversian «Sechser» (2 + 2 + 2), but a Qinah, as are the other «stichoi» of this psalm. But the first colon is a little too long; *meçulå* is a gloss to *bilebab yammim*, as is seen from the lack of the preposition.

Archaistically formed tricola Albright (*op.cit.* p. 8) finds also in the psalm **Hab. 3:2b, 4, 6b, 7, 8**. I have discussed the interpretation and the text of Hab. 3 in my paper in *ThZ* IX. *V. 2c* and *d* are simply doublets, the former is the better one; s. op.cit. p. 6,9f. — V. 6e has the theme: Yahweh's coming (epiphany) in common with v. 4—5, while already v. 6a describes the results of his coming; accordingly v. 6e must be replaced after v. 4c. Both v. 4 and v. 6 thus get 4 cola (2 bicola) each. V. 4, 6e builds one stanza, vv. 5a, b, 6a, b another. — A closer description of the said results is given in the next stanza, vv. 6c, d, 7a, b; as for the text v. 7 see *op.cit.* p. 14, partly in accordance with Albright. — V. 8 cannot

be a «repetitive tricolon»; in a disjunctive *ha-'im* clause, there must
be two *different* alternatives, but the questions in 8a and b are
identical; *'im ban-nehárim* must be deleted and *yhwh* placed behind
bay-yám; v. 8 thus becomes a regular Mashal bicolon (*op.cit.* p. 15).

c) *In the other cases exegetical considerations lead to the result
that some words or a colon must have been lost in TM.*
Considering the history of the transmission of the O.T. texts
from the first oral stage to the literary fixation and the repeated
copying by more or less «learned» scribes, often from more or less
mutilated mss. it is unavoidable that we must reckon with larger
or smaller lacunae in the text. In fact, I think that this is the solution
of more exegetical and textual cruces than the suggestion of secondary glosses, doublets or the like. To take only one instance:
in **56:14** certainly nothing is to be omitted, a simple and stylistic
adequate *le'olám* at the end gives 2 regular Mashal bicola, just
what we here have to expect. — How easily the scribe can omit one
or more words e.g. by homoioteleuton, one can see by comparing
the Hebrew text of Samuel with the text of G, the far-reaching
superiority of which has been clearly demonstrated by H. Tiktin.[1]

That in fact, a whole bicolon or two may have been lost in the
Massoretic text of the Psalms, can with absolute certainty be demonstrated from the acrostich of the «alphabetic» psalms (s. above
§ 6). So we with certainty can say thàt in Ps. 9, between vv. 6 and
7, the whole Daleth-stanza, 2 bicola, are lost; in Ps. 10, between
vv. 2 and 3, the first bicolon of the Mem-stanza is lost — all the
other textual corruptions in this psalm apart. In Ps. 34, between
vv. 6 and 7, the Waw bicolon is lacking, and in Ps. 145, between
vv. 13 and 14, the Nun-bicolon.

There is no reason to believe, that these are all the cases
concerned. We have seen above (§ 4) that there are not a few cases

---

[1] H. Tiktin, *Kritische Untersuchungen zu den Büchern Samuelis*, Göttingen, 1922. — The Qumran finds have given us some fragments of a
Hebrew Samuel text which in many places is in accordance with G, not
with TM. See Frank M. Cross, Jr., «A New Qumran Biblical Fragment
Related to the Original Hebrew Underlying the Septuaqint», *BASOR* 132,
1953, pp. 15ff; cf. the same in *BASOR* 141, 1956, pp. 9ff.

where a colon has been lost in the Hebrew text, which is found in G or some other old translation.

Thus there may be instances where a colon or a bicolon (or more) has been lost without having left any trace in any of the text witnesses known to us.

That this really is the fact, can often with all probability be demonstrated both by the «law of parallelism» and by exegetical considerations. We shall now discuss some apparent «tricola», where this irregularity obviously is due to omissions by the copyist, or perhaps already to a slip of memory in the oral transmission.

5:13b «thou crownest him as a shield», or «as with a shield» (AV) is nonsense; it is obvious that a predicate fitting the comparison «as a shield» has been lost. By supplementing such a word, e.g. *wetåsek 'ålemo* from v. 12, v. 13b gets meaning, and appears to consist of a regular Qinah.

Then, to be sure, we expect v. 13a to be one, as well; a word telling *with what* the Lord blesses «the right man», is wished for; a *baššålom* (BHK) should make the line complete.

12:6 at least a subject to *yåfi^aḥ* is missed. But then v. 6c becomes too long for an ordinary colon; thus more than a single word has been lost. Nothing then prevents the conjecture that v. 6 originally had two full bicola, and that v. 6c once may have had something like *'åni wådal* (hendiadyoin) *'ašær råšå'*.

A fragment of an older psalm is included by the poet in **19:2—7**, cpr. p. 47 to Ps. 144:14ff. This older psalm has been written in Mashal metre, as against the Qinah metre in the late poet's own product vv. 8ff. The Mashal metre of vv. 2—7 seems to have been regularily bicolic. With v. 7c the fragment is interrupted; nothing prevents the suggestion that it once has had its parallel colon; according to the «law of duality» (see above p. 6) this is very probable. The same may be said, and with still greater probability, about v. 5c. In the present context the tent, where the Sun enters in the evening, having ended its *tequfå*, is situated in the heavens, as the plural suffix in *båhæm*, as the text now runs, can only go back to *haššå-mayim* v. 2. But undoubtedly this word stands rather far away. And when we consider the old cosmology, the Sun in the evening

goes down in the sea, and, at least according to Egyptian mytho-
logy, crosses the subterranean ocean in its boat. According to the
geographical situation of Palestine, the Sun even goes down in the
western sea, beneath the horizon. We may therefore suppose that
in Palestinian mythological cosmology, the tent of the Sun is
situated in the sea. Accordingly some words before v. 5a must have
been lost, among which was the word *bayyammim;* to this word,
then, the suffix in *båhæm* points. It may be mentioned that commentators long ago proposed to read *bayyåm* or *bit͏ᵉhom* instead
of *båhæm*, s. BHK.

At all events, v. 5 is no real «tricolon», v. 5c is in relation to
v. a,b a new factor in the description, no third «membrum» parallel
v. a,b.

Some might be inclined to find a tricolon in **21:10**, see e.g.
Baethgen, *Die Psalmen*³, Göttingen 1904, p. 61, who, however,
thinks v. c to be secondary. At all events *yhwh* must be deleted;
the psalm speaks about the King, not about Yahweh, but it has
in later use been re-interpreted on Y., and this word is a gloss
expressing this re-interpretation. A witness of the original text is
G's *beʾappekå teballeʿem*, obviously correct. *tśytmw* is but an irregular
orthography for *tçytmw = taççitemo* (BHK). The expression *leʿet
pånækæ*, however, is an awkward one; the meaning becomes clearer
and the wording more natural if we read *leʿet harʾotåm ʾæt pånækå*.
If so, we have here a full bicolon, v. 10a,b. The rest *beʾappekå* etc.
is no third colon of a tricolon, but a verse with its own inner parallelism, in fact a Mashal bicolon, v. 10c,d. The unqualified *ʾeš* is,
however, scarcely correct; the context shows that the poet does not
speak about a naturalistic «fire», but about the metaphorical fire
of the king's wrath; we certainly have to read *ʾeš haronekå*.

That the interpretation v. 10 as two bicola is correct, is corroborated by the fact that the psalm then appears as being built
up of 2 uniform stanzas, 7 Mashal bicola to each: vv. 2—8 the
congregation's intercession for the King, speaking of him in 3. pers.
vv. 9—14, the word of blessing, spoken to the King in 2. pers.

Apparently **22:27** is a tricolon. As mentioned above (p. 40)
the psalm seems to be built up of stanzas of 3 bicola each. At all

events vv. 26—27 from the viewpoint of content belong together, a stanza dealing with the future thanksgiving psalm and the paying of the vows, of which «the meek» then are going to eat together with the worshipper; with v. 28 a new thought begins. The stanza vv. 26—27 consists of 2½ bicolon instead of the expected 3. But v. 26a, in fact, is rather long for a single colon. The parallel colon to v. 26b is v. 27a: the paying of the vows ⧺ the eating thereof. Accordingly, v. 27b and c belong together, forming the next bicolon; v. 27c obviously is the standing formula with which the sacrificer (Accad. *bêl nikêti*) invites the guests to come and take part in the sacrificial meal, cpr. 69:33, where the same formula is taken up in a similar text. — If so, then we must assume that some words have fallen out in v. 26a, and that it originally has made a full bicolon.

We turn again to **Ps. 29**, this time *v. 3—4*. We have seen above, that the metre in vv. 1—2 is not a $2 + 2$ beat, but a $4 + 4$ beat metre. It is easy to see that we have the same metre in vv. 5—6, 8, 9a, 9c, 10—11 as well. And as the introit in vv. 1—2 makes a «stanza», a metrically and logically well-rounded distinct section of its own so do the vv. 5—6 and 10—11 respectively. This does, it seems reasonable to suppose, show that the whole psalm was built up of such stanzas. — In v. 3 begins the corpus of the hymn, the *tehillot* for which the poet wants to praise and extol Yahweh. The first theme is His victory over the Sea through his wonderful «voice», vv. 3—4. The next theme is His voice in the thunderstorm, breaking the cedars of Lebanon and making Siryon dance as a buffalo calf. V. 5 starts a new theme and is logically connected with v. 6. — It thus is quite unjustified when Albright (*op.cit.* p. 6) takes «4f» as one metrical unity according to the pattern «abc | abd ‖ ab | ef». The bigger metrical unity, the stanza next after vv. 1—2 are the vv. 3—4. In TM they build a tricolon and a bicolon, while we expect two bicola. It is, however, easy to see that in v. 3, with its clumsy syntax and word sequence, the text cannot be in order. When all the (apparent) three cola are to be directed by same verb (*hir'im*), we at least expect to find this in the first. There can be little doubt that the original text was something like this

> qol yhwh 'al ham-mayim hir'im
> 'el hak-kâbod 'al mayim rabbim —

a perfect 4 + 4 bicolon. It was just in this struggle with the waters of chaos that His voice appeared in activity as being *beko^{a}ḥ* and *behadâr*, v. 4. The poet will not tell about Yahweh's voice, as to its habitus and permanent quality, but what by this special opportunity it showed itself to be, what it just then was, in actual activity. That is just what the Hebrew expresses through the verb *hâyâ*. This predicate cannot be missed in v. 4; the original text must have had: *hâyâ bakko^{a}ḥ, hâyâ bæhâdâr* (probably to vocalize without article). — Again a perfect 4 + 4 bicolon. How *hyh* can have fallen out behind *yhwh* can easily be imagined.

The same metre as in vv. 1—2 Albright also finds in «vv. 7f», i.e. vv. 7—8 (*op. cit.* p. 6). But TM *v. 7*: «The voice of the Lord divideth the flames of fire» (AV), is simply nonsense; «divide flames of fire» every man can do; that is no worthy deed for which to praise Yahweh. «The flames of fire» are obviously the means by which Yahweh splits something; the verb *ḥobeç* must have an object. The old conjecture

qól yahwǽ ḥobéç çurím (or: *selâʿim*)

wayyáḥsebém beláh^{a}bot^1-ʾés (BHK),

or something like that, is quite obviously on the right track. This being so, vv. 7—8 form a stanza of two 4 + 4 bicola.

There remains *v. 9*. When the psalm is built up of distichs, more than one colon seems to be missing; TM gives only 2½ four beat cola. An insertion of a *qol yhwh* in v. 9b (and then: *yeḥassef*) commends itself in view of the thorough going use of this catchword. At all events, some words are missing, for now there is no factual and logical connection between v. b and c; why should just the special effect of Yahweh's voice in v. a,b result in the heavenly acclamation in v. c? Obviously v. 9c rounds off the theme announced in the «introitus»: the homage of the *bene ʾelim* in the heavenly palace. It seems very probable that this thought must have been more fully expressed than in v. 9c, which now comes very abruptly. As v. 9c brings a quite new thought in relation to v. a,b, it is not easily possible to take it as a third colon in a tricolon; in the real tricolon the three cola are organically connected with each other and build a more or less close parallelism (see above pp. 17ff).

---

[1] See above p. 33 n. 1.

But then the «law of duality» makes it very probable that a colon, parallel 9c has been lost, as have some words in 9b. If this be so, even v. 9 has originally had two 4 + 4 bicola.

32:8b AV translates «I will guide thee with mine eye». That is very unsatisfactory. *yāʿaç* does not mean «guide», but «advise, give counsel», abs. or with inner obj. *ʿeçâ;* constructed with *lĕ* or with *ʿeçâ* and obj. it means «advise a person«, with *ʿal:* «on account of» the thing or case in question. TM must be translated: I will give advice on account of thee; but the interpretation of *ʿeni* as a *beʿeni* is rather daring. — G has *ʾæ°ᵃçæ, √ˉāçâ*, cpr. Prov. 16:30: «I will fix mine eye upon thee». That is obviously the only interpretation which fits the object *ʿeni* and the preposition «upon thee». But this correction does not suffice; the fixing of the eye upon one is only an introductory gest; the following verses indicate undoubtedly that the worshipper = the person who offers his thanksoffering and recites this thanksgiving psalm, here wants to give someone, i.e. the congregation that celebrates the occasion together with him, an admonition and advice from his own experience; that is just what the «witness» in the thanksgiving psalm does. So the context demands *both* readings, TM as well as G:

$$\text{ʾæ°ᵃçæ ʿâlǽkâ ʿeni} \quad | \quad \text{weʾiᶜaçâ lekâ.}$$

We thus get a full Qinah, parall. v. 8a.

In **35:17** *hǎšibâ* is not the right verb for the thought in v. b TM; the «soul» may be «brought back» from Sheol, or from the state of impotence, debility or death; from «the destructions» (AV) of the enemies («their») and «the lions», however, it must be «saved», «delivered», «taken away», *hiççil* or some other synonym. *hǎšibâ nafši*, therefore, must be connected with the foregoing words, being the shorter second colon of the Qinah verse, and a *wehiççileni* supplemented before *miššoʾehæm* (read: *miššoʾagim*, BHK).

50:7. The poetical and liturgical scene in this psalm is analogous with that in 81: Yahweh's epiphany followed by his reproach and his admonition to the people; s. above p. 49, and *Offersang og Sangoffer* pp. 156, 161, 324ff, 546. To the idea of the cultic epiphany belongs the self-introduction «I am Y. thy God» and the reference to the basic dead of salvation, the exodus. Then there is all reason to fill up v. 7c from 81:11b: *hamma͑ᵃlekå meˀæræç miçråyim*.

In **59:8** obviously something has fallen out, behind the 3 first words *ki mi šome͑ᵃᶜ*, which now stand without any logical connection. If we are right in our opinion that the psalm is built up of regular stanzas, 2 Mashal bicola to the stanza, almost 2 bicola have been lost. That something is missing is corroborated by the observation that even in v. 7 a bicolon = v. 16 must have fallen out; it is not reasonable, that the poet only should have repeated the first half of the description vv. 15—16.

That some words are lacking in vv. **12—14** too, is seen i.a. from the fact that a verb is missing in v. 13a. A lover of irregularity may find tricola in all these verses; the way of dividing the lines in BHK only makes things still more obscure. Logically v. 12a ends with *͑ammi*, TM is right in letting a relatively new form of the thought begin with v. 13. — In v. 12 we of course must pronounce *ˀeli* for *ˀal*, the suffix refers to the enemies; the second colon begins with *pæn*, some words are lacking, i.a. an object, saying *what* «my people» not may forget; then we are entitled to suppose that a word or two is lost in the first colon as well, e.g. *beˀappekå*, or *běkohĕkå*, cpr. *běhelĕka* 12b. — In v. 12b read *hakni͑emo* (BHK); the second colon *måginnenu* etc. is incomplete, syntactically and logically; obviously something like *ki ˀattå* must be supplemented before *måginnenu*. — In v. 13a the first clause at least a verb, coord. *weyillåkedu*, is lacking; the two parallel nouns indicate the loss of two predicates e.g. something like *habcˀ ͑ålemo* and *šallem ͑alemo*. — A new complete bicolon v. 13b begins with *yillåkedu*. — In v. 14 a (second) bicolon begins with *weycde͑u* (so correctly BHK). V. 14a is incomplete; to the transitive verb *kallc* we expect an object; in accordance with *běhelekå* in v. 12 we also expect a *baḫᵃmåtĕkå* instead of the naked *běhåmå*, the thought rhyme (parallelism) seems to indicate that the two *kalle* represent two different cola. One night suppose something like: *kalle-[mo yhwh] baḫᵃmåtĕkå/ kalle[mo] weˀenemo [båˀåræç]*.

The following lines may give an approximate conception of the original wording:

[12]*eli tahargém [bekóhekā (?)],*
pæn yiškehú ʿammi [. . . .],
hákniʿémo behéleká,
[ki ʾattā] māginnènú[1] yahwǽ.

[13][*habéʾ ʿalémo*] *háttaʾt[2]-pímo,*
[*šallém ʿalémo*] *dēbár šēfātémo,*
wĕyíllākĕdú bigéʾonám
meʾālā umik-káhaš yĕsáppĕrú.

[14]*kallé[mo yahwǽ] bahᵃmā[teká],*
kallé[mo] wᵉʾenémo [ʿód bāʾáræç],
weyédeʿú ki [ʾattá] ʾælóhim
mošél beyaʿᵃqób lᵉafsé hāʾáræç.

The uncertainty of these emendations admitted, so much at least seems clear, that we have to do with bicola, not with tricola. Corroboration may be seen in the fact that by this analysis of the text the vv. 12—14 make 3 regular «basic stanzas», in accordance with the metrical structure of the other parts of the psalm.

But what about v. 18? To say the least: this verse is no real tricolon; the vocative at the end *ʾælohe hasdi* is too short for a real colon. — Obviously, the verse must be supplemented after v. 11, as suggested in BHK; probably we have not to do here with a accidental lacuna, but with an abbreviation by the scribe; what he has meant, is: «*ʾælohe hasdi*, etc. as in v. 11».

61:3 is an apparent tricolon, but v. c is grammatically in-correct. One translates «lead me to a rock that is higher than me» (AV), better would be «a rock too high for me». But when *náhā*, Hiph. *hinhā* is constructed with *be*, this does not denote the goal to which one leads, but the road or the terrain on which one leads (67:5 is no exception). The goal is denoted by *ʾæl* (orthographically incorrect: *ʿal*), s. 107:30; Job 38:32. This leads to the conclusion that either the reading of G *terememeni* must be correct, or a verb

---

[1] See above p. 25 n. 1. Or perhaps with retraction of the accent in *ʾattā:*
ki ʾátta máginnénu Yahwǽ.

[2] See above p. 33 n. 1.

constructed with *be* must have fallen out before *beçur*. At all events
the line, then, is too long for a single colon; before *tanḥeni* a parallel
word to *çur* is lost. Then v. 3c, originally, has consisted of 2 Qinah
bicola.

66 is, as we have seen above (p. 27) built up of regular bicolic
Mashal verses, two bicola making a stanza. Only vv. 12 and 16
seem to be exceptions. *V. 12*, however, is obviously mutilated;
lårewåyå is not the word expected behind *wattoçi'enu*, first the
deliverance (being «brought out») to freedom, and then the happy
life in «abundance». Read

       wattóçi'énu [lår°wåḥå | wattébi'énu] lår°wåyå.

— Thus there is reason to believe that even in *v. 16* a colon may
have been lost before (or behind) v. c. According to the stylistic
rules of the thanksgiving psalm, *kol yir'e 'ælohim* is a vocative,
not a remote object to be connected with *wa'asapperå*, in the latter
case we should expect *lekol*. But the logical place of the vocative
would be behind *šim'u*. This seems to indicate a certain disorder
in the transmission of the text. The possibility may, however, be
admitted, that v. 16 as the introduction to the «record» proper
of the thanksgiving psalm, vv. 17—19, even originally may have
had a form of its own, not conforming to the strophic structure
of the psalm.

We again turn to **73:28**. As we have seen above p. 33 it is
manifest that TM has lost 1 colon that is preserved in G. The
possibility at least is given, that more has been lost. Now it is clear
that something is wrong also with v. 26. The verse is no right
bicolon of the common type; v. b is too long, no matter whether
one tries to scan it according to Sievers' system or any other metrical
system, especially in this psalm, where the other bicola are of the
regular symmetric type (a and b of the same length). On the other
hand v. 26 is no tricolon; it does not consist of three «membra»,
which in some or other way are «parallel» to each other. The verse
is overloaded, and the words which appoint themselves as not
original in this connection, are *çur lebabi*. But how have they come
in here? Labelling as «a gloss» only does not solve any problem.
Here the fact that some words have been lost in v. 28 will be taken

in consideration. According to the meaning *çur lebåbi* is the same as *maḥasi* v. 28b. Is it too daring to suppose, that before v. 28b a parallel colon has been lost, of which the *çur lebåbi* is a displaced remnant? E.g. *wå'ættĕnehu çur lebåbi*. *šatti* then begins a new bicolon, the last consists of 28c and the plus in G. — If this be so, v. 28a remains alone, but is too short for a regular bicolon. Now the worshipper's express declaration of his intention to thank Yahweh is a consistent element in the thanksgiving psalms; it may have its place at the beginning, but usually it stands at the end, after the narrative about the experiences of the worshipper. This intention is hinted at in v. 28c *lesapper* etc. But the express declaration is now missing. Again: is it too daring to suppose that some pertinent words have been lost in v. 28a, after *wa'ani*, e.g. *'odæ 'æt yhwh*? This should make the bicolon full.

The original wording of vv. 27—28 may have been something like this:

> [27]*kí hinné reheqǽkå yo'bédu,*
>   *hiçmåttå kól-zonǽ mimmǽkå,*
> [28]*wa'ªní* [*'odǽ 'æt šém yahwǽ*],
>   *qírbat 'ælohím li-ṭób.*

> *šátti bå'ªdonåy mahªsí*
>   *wå'ættenéhu çúr lebåbi,*
> *lesápper[1] kôl-nífl°otékå*
>   *bešá'arê bát çiyyón.*

If one approve the above proposals, one will see that also Ps. 73, as so many others, is built up of the small «basic stanzas» to 2 bicola each. The next last consists of v. 27 and the reconstructed v. 28a; the last of the rest of the reconstructed v. 28b, ɔ: *šatti* etc.

90:17 consists even in TM of 2 bicola; in so far BHK is wrong in printing *uma'aśe* etc. on the same line as the foregoing words. The first bicolon reaching to *'alenu*[1], is, however, a little too short; The second, *ma'aśe yådenu* etc. is in disorder; it cannot have been the intention of the poet to give a bicolon, with two identical cola; if it had been, he would hot have repeated the word *'alenu*[2], which has no logical connection at all, neither with the foregoing clause

---

[1] See above p. 33 n. 1.

nor with following one — that God may establish, or make steadfast, the work of our hands «upon us» or «over us», is nonsense; a *lånu* would give better sense. The scribe has simply repeated the second last colon + the foregoing word, and overlooked the original, last colon. To this error it also may be due, that the first bicolon is now too short; a word or two have been lost after *ʿalenu*[1], e.g. *ledor wådor*, cpr. v. 2.

As we have seen above p. 28, **95:7b** must be connected with vv. 8ff. After the hymn of praise (enthronement hymn) vv. 1—5 and the expression of the congregation's decision to come and bow down and worship their Creator, God, and Shepherd vv. 6—7a, v. 7b opens the second part of the liturgy, the divine admonition before the renewal of the covenant, see the parallel Ps. 81. A real tricolon is neither v. 7 nor vv. 7b + 8. — But there are real reasons to think that the psalm is fragmentary. Compared with the parallel Ps. 81, essential elements of the presupposed liturgical context seem to be missing. The cultic background of the admonition (and the renewal of the covenant) vv. 7cff is the epiphany of the God, and, accordingly, his admonition regularly starts with his self-introduction, s. 50:7; 81:11. And as abruptly as the admonition now starts, just so abruptly it ends; we expect a continuation, like that in 81:15ff; 132:12cff: not only the reproach, but also the promise; both these elements belong to the cultic idea of the renewal of the convenant, which is the background of both of them, and both of them were expressed in the liturgical realization of the idea. — 95:7 then gives no basis for speaking about tricolic verses. — Nor does v. *10; bedor* needs a closer determination, at least a *haz-zæ*, and thus at all events becomes too long for a single colon. Here, too, we have to do with a fragmentary text.

In **109:21e** G has a longer text: *berob* before *ḥasdekå;* there is no reason why this should not be original. But TM must have lost more words also not found in G. TM «for good is thy [great] kindness» gives no good sense here. What we expect in this context is a cry for help and an appeal to Yahweh's great kindness and goodness. The first colon *weʾattå yhwh ʾadonåy* has no predicate; a nominal clause: «and thou art Y. the Lord» would not fit the context, and is scarcely intended by the poet. Read *re'eni* instead of *'adonây*. For the missing words in v. c, we may suppose *zokreni* and *'attâ*, read

[*zokréni*] *kí* [*'attâ*] *tôb*

berób ḥasdékâ[1] *háççiléni*.

In **116:16a** quite obviously a predicate is missing before *ki*, the line is incomplete, a word or two have been lost, e.g. *hoši'a-nnâ* or the like; cpr. 118:25. In all probability this line, too, originally has been a Qinah, cpr. below p. 84.

In **118:12a**, too, it is clear that some words have been lost. There is no pertinent and logical correspondance between the predicate *do'aku* «they blazed» and the metaphor of the bees, *kaddeborim*, the characteristic of the bees is not that they «blaze», but that they «swarm» or the like. So it is obvious that a verb telling what the enemies did «like the bees», is lost, and, likewise, a sentence telling under what circumstances «they», i.e. the enemies «blazed». This being so, there can be no doubt that among these lost words has also been the refrain of the two stanzas vv. 10f and 12: *bešem yhwh ki 'amilem*. That means: v. 12 originally was not a tricolon, but a stanza of 2 bicola, just as vv. 10f.

8.

In all the cases dealt with in § 7 more or less evident exegetical reasons have indicated that the text of TM has not been in order. The metrical arguments have had a more secondary place in our consideration, even if they in some cases have been appealed to as auxiliary arguments. But very often the metrical structure has corroborated the exegetical results, as these vice versa, ofte haven let the original and intended regularity of the metrical organization become apparent. One result of the above enquiries is in my opinion that the metrical structures as a rule are much more regular than often supposed. This would appear much more evident if we had reviewed the many cases where a regular metrical and strophic organization of the poem is obvious and indisputable without any critical operations.

---

[1] We may take it as a plural, or scan: *berôb hàsdekấ*.

In the light of these recognitions it seems not unjustified when in this paragraph we want to deal with cases where the *metrical regularity* that rules the other verses or stanzas of a psalm, becomes the main argument against accepting an apparent tricolon.

As we have seen (§ 5, 7b), there are not few cases where other text-witnesses prove that some words, a text-variant, a dittography, at gloss or the like, have been inserted in the TM text. As a rule, this result has been corroborated by metrical observations. This proves the possibility that such secondary elements can be found even in cases where no other text-witnesses are at hand.

a) First some *dittographies*.

To these we may safely count **27:14a** = v. 14c. *Ps. 27* is built up of regular Qinah stichs (bicola), the Massoretic verse division and the division of the lines in BHK is partly wrong. V. 6c,d make 1 Qinah (del. *be'ohlo*, and *'ăširâ*), v. 8a another, vv. 8b, 9a a third. As most of the verses of this psalm are clear Qinoth, there is good reason to believe that the shorter half of a Qinah has been lost after *darkækå* v. 11 (s. BHK). — In *v. 12a* Hie testifies that at least a *yhwh* has been lost; so this line, too, may have been a regular Qinah. — Two and two Qinah bicola make a stanza; on the only exeption v. 4 see below p. 72. V. 4b, however, is in all probability a later addition, a generalizing sentence without any clear reference to the actual occasion of the psalm and the situation of the worshipper. Under these circumstances there is every reason to believe that the repetition of v. 14c in 14a is secondary.

The verse **35:25** is in BHK printed as a Qinah bicolon and, on the next line, a single colon, which, however, the editor takes as a variant or a gloss to the first colon in v. a. This seems probable as long as one is bound by the Sieversian conception of the nature of the Qinah $(3 + 2)$; having realized its true nature $(4 + 3)$, however, one sees that v. a is rather short for a Qinah. Moreover, *billa'nuhu* seems necessary for the full expression of the thought. If we take the second *'al yo'meru* as an erroneous dittography, the Qinah is restored:

'al yŏ'mĕrú belíbbåtåm | nafšénu billa'núhu.

The words *millåšon remiyyå* in **120:2** are in all probability only a simple dittography of the same words in v. 3, NB the Qinah metre; v. 5b is a little too long, but *šåkanti* may be secondary, cpr. BHK.

A simple dittography is almost certainly **131:2c**. When these words are deleted, the psalm appears as consisting of 2 regular stanzas, 2 Qinah bicola to each stanza.

The text of **Isa. 38**, the thanksgiving psalm of Hizqiyah, is, as well known, transmitted in a very bad condition, but has been brilliantly reconstructed by J. Begrich, in accordance with the principles of the «Gattungsforschung» (*Der Psalm des Hiskia*, *FRLANT* 42, Göttingen 1926). Here *v. 12* consists of 2 Qinah bicola and a 5th colon v.e. The latter is, however, verbotim identical with v. 13c, which is undoubtedly only an erroneous dittography of v. 12e. V. 12e obviously must be connected with the short v. 13a, thus making a regular Qinah; v. 13b is in fact a whole Qinah, the second in this verse and «basic stanza». See Begrich *ad loc.* and BHK.

b) *Another group of apparent tricola is in fact but a result of a combination of two variants that have been taken up in the text of TM* — variants that represent different text-types or schools of tradition.

A variant to the preceding words is in all probability Ps. **13:3b**. When deleted, the four *'ad-'ånå* vv. 2a, 2b, 3a, 3c correspond exactly to each other and make a basic stanza, as do the vv. 4— 5 and 6 respectively (on v. 6 see above § 4, p. 32).

A text-variant, and no independent single colon, is in all probability **20:6c**; the line says nothing that is not already said in v. 5. — Another possibility is to take the line as a sort of refrain or chorus, see below § 9b. Without this line the psalm consists of 2 quite regular stanzas, 5 bicola to each.

In this group belong also **40:10—11**. On vv. 7—9 see above p. 25f. The whole section vv. 7—11 contains the vow of the worshipper. In v. 7—9 he speaks about the less valuable way of thanksgiving: the sacrifice of animals, and of the true way of thanking

God: by obedience to what is written in the book scroll. In vv.
10—11 he speaks about the thanksgiving song in the congregation,
the prevalent form of the vow in the psalms. The vv. 10—11 now
seem to be two tricola, the latter v. 11, however, a very bad one,
betok libbi making the apparent second colon between the two long
cola 11a and 11c. Commentators often have been offended by the
— as it seems — quite unnecessary repetitions in these two verses.
V. 11a *biśśarti çædæq beqåhål råb* is = v. 11aα + cβ *çidqåtekå lo'kissiṭi
...leqåhål råb* = v. 11cα *lo' kiḥadti ḥasdekå wa'amittekå leqåhål råb*. It
seems very probable that v. 10 and v. 11 are but variants of the
same stanza, the one line of which is transmitted in three variant
forms. That at least a suffix has been lost after *çædæq* v. 10 is obvious.
If we suppose that v. 10 must be filled up after v. 11b: *biśśarti
['æmunåtekå we]çidqekå*, and v. 11a after v. 11c: *çidqekå [weḥasdekå]
lo'kissiti* etc., and take v. 11c as a variant to v. 11a, we shall have
two complete stanzas, two Qinah verses to the stanza:

[10]*biśśarti ['æmunåtekå / we]çidqekå beqåhål-råb
hinne śefåtay lo' 'æklå / yhwh 'attå yådå'ti.*

[11]*çidqekå [weḥasdekå] / lo' kissiti betok libbi,
'æmunåtekå uteśu'åtekå / 'åmarti[0] leqåhål-råb.*

It seems very improbable that the poet should have repeated
himself in this way; we have to do with two variants of the same
original «text».

69:36c. The stanzas of this psalm contain mostly 3 Qinah
verses each; an exception is v. 4; apparently also vv. 26—29, but
v. 27 breaks the context between v. 26 and v. 28f and is a Mashal
bicolon, no Qinah; it may be a quotation from an other psalm.
— V. 36 is apparently a tricolon, but no real one; v.c has no real
logical connexion with v. a,b, grammatically «they» in *weyåśebu*
should be «Zion and the cities of Judah», but that would be nonsense.
V. c is almost certainly only a variant of v. 37b, as suggested in BHK.

77:2b. The second part of this psalm vv. 2—13 (s. above p. 16),
is built up of Mashal bicola, 3 bicola to a stanza. V. 2b then most
probably is only a variant of v. a. The second part vv. 14—21 is
tricolic.

At **78:21** one may be in doubt whether a colon has been lost after v. a, or v. c is a variant of v. b. I prefer the latter solution, but am not able to give decisive grounds for it. — A variant is in all probability *v. 71c*. The metre is regular Mashal bicola.

In all probability we have to do with text-variants in **79:13**. The metre of the psalm is the Mashal (*mâher* v. 8 must be replaced before ʿ*ozreni* v. 9); the rhythm is very often anapaestic instead of jambic. In such surroundings v. 13b *nodæ lekå leʿolåm* is much too short to make a colon for itself. The words are probably a variant of 13c.

106:5c is a variant of v. b. The metre of the psalm is the Mashal bicolon; two bicola make a stanza, the simple «basic stanza». (V. 3 must be replaced before v. 6, and is the antithetic introduction to the confession of sins in vv. 6ff.)

The inner logic of the conception in **109:18—19** — the Nessus shirt! — shows that v. 19b must be put before v. 18b: may he put on the curse as a shirt (18a) and as a girdle he continually wears (19b), so that it (the curse) intrudes upon his entrails and all his limbs (v. 18b)! Then it becomes quite clear that v. 18a and 19a are variants; v. 18a is the better, since it expressly mentions the curse, *qelålå*, as subject. Vv. 17, 18a, 19b then make 2 bicola, vv. 18b,c, 20 the 2 following ones, and the apparent tricola disappear.

116:3 is an apparent tricolon. V. 3c says in prosaic words what a,b say in a mythical picture, the meaning of which is quite clear; 3c is in so far superfluous. V. 3a and b are the corresponding membra of the parallelism, both of them mentioning the real enemy: Death, She'ol. V. 3c is a weaker variant. — On the metre s. below p. 84.

In all probability **123:4b** and **4c** are only text-variants. The assumed 3rd colon contains absolutely nothing but a repetition of the second in synonymous words. Apart from v. 4c the psalm is made up of quite regular Qinah stichs (bicola), 2 and 2 making a «basic stanza». There is neither a logical nor an esthetical reason to repeat the two last words.

On the metrical structure of **143** see above p. 29. According to this it seems very probable that v. *5b* and *5c* are text-variants.

c) *In other apparent tricola the assumed 3rd colon is in all probability only explanatory glosses.*

27:4. As we have seen above (p. 68) this psalm is built up of regular «basic stanzas» in Qinah metre. The only exception is v. 4 with three Qinah stichoi (bicola). V. 4b, however, is in all probability a later addition, a generalizing sentence without any clear reference to the actual occasion of the psalm and the situation of the worshipper. On v. 14 see above p. 68.

35:8a. The psalm is built up of normal basic stanzas, 2 bicola — here Qinah verses — to the stanza. On vv. 16—17, see above p. 61. V. 7 is a stanza for itself, vv. 8b, c, 9 another. It seems rather obvious that v. 8a is an explanatory prose gloss to the metaphors in v. 7. — On v. 25 see p. 68.

39:5c. The psalm is built up on the same scheme as 35. On vv. 6b, 7a see above p. 25. Under these circumstances it is very probable that v. 5c is an explanatory gloss to v. 5b.

49:9—11,15. The metre of this psalm is the Mashal bicolon. At some places, however, the metrical pattern is blurred. V. 9 might be read as a rather bad Qinah verse; v. 10, too, is too short, and so is v. 12b; v. 11 seems to be a tricolon, and even v. 15 consists of three stichoi, but all of them are too long for a normal four-beat colon.

As v. 9 now stands TM rightly takes it as a parenthesis, and lets v. 10 syntactically continue v. 8. But the first words of v. 10 obviously are corrupt; instead of *'od* both parallelism and logic demands a «for ever», parall. *lånæçæḥ; le'olåm* v. 9 must be taken to v. 10, the text emended: *wiḥi le'olåm wå'åd*, and Athnach replaced from *næçaḥ* to *'åd*, see BHK. Then it becomes clear that the rest of v. 9 is an explanatory prose gloss to vv. 8, 10: «the redemption of their souls should be (too) precious, and he must give up (to try for any such redemption)». — In v. 11a,b read *'ær'æ* for *yir'æ*, and *wenåbon* for *wåba'ar* (BHK), and in v. 12a *qirbåm* (G, S, T). V. 12c has no logical connection with v. 12a,b. We expect to hear something expressly about «those who call lands after their own names», i.e., took lands in possession. It seems rather clear, that the two isolated cola v. 11c and v. 12c belong together, and that v.

12c must be replaced before v. 11c: «(even) they must leave their wealth to others». — In v. 14b read *wa'aharitâm pihæm yâruçu* (cpr. T, A H⁰, Hie, se BHK): «such is the way (i.e. fate) of those (who walk) in stupid security, the end of those, whose mouths run (haughtily)». V. 15 then explains more in detail their bad fate. The text of TM, however, is altogether unclear, if not to say, logically and syntactically nonsense, and no doubt corrupted: «like sheep they have set, death shall herd them, the upright trampled upon them in the morning, and their rock, to let them disappear (in) She'ol away from (i. e. so there is no) dwelling (or: highness) for him». I read:

> *kaççô'n liše'ól [yeléku] / ubéšibţô mâwæt yir'ém*
> *yeredú bamm̂éšârim laq-qǣbær / ⁰še'ól le'olâm zebûl lâm,*

and delete *weçurâm:*

> Like sheep they must go to She'ol,
>> where Death herds them with his staff,
> they must go the straight way down to the grave,
>> She'ol is their house (or: palace) for ever.

In v. 19 read *yodukâ* (without *we*). Thus reconstructed — and v. 21 preliminarily left alone — the psalm appears to be built up of equal stanzas, 4 Mashal bicola to a stanza. Then it also becomes clear that v. 21 = v. 13 is no real refrain; if so, we should expect, that like v. 13, it should either make the fourth bicolon of its stanza, or divide the psalm in two equal parts. V. 21 is, in fact, but a secondary addition, motivated by the similarity between vv. 12 and 20.

50:3 is no real tricolon, v. 3a is an isolated colon without any formal connection with 3b,c. In fact, it interrupts the close connection between vv. 1—2 and 3b,c, the description of the theophany. — The direct continuation of v. 2 is v. 3b,c, the closer explanation of the *hofi'ᵃᶜ* v. 2: as he shines forth, fire devours before him, round about him the tempest rages mightily. Here the voluntative clause, the wish or prayer: «may our God come and not keep silence!» is quite out of place. The psalm tells that God really comes, scil. in the cultic epiphany, and how his coming is experienced there by the congregation; through the mouth of the cult prophet he then says what he has to say, vv. 5ff. V. 3a is a wishful sigh out of an eschatological interpretation of the psalm, a marginal note by some copyist or reader, who is no longer aware of the original cultic meaning of the psalm.

56:10 is in BHK printed as two lines, but, as BHK itself suggests, *beyom 'æqrâ'* is but a superfluous gloss to *'âz*, taken from v. 4. Without these words the verse makes a normal Mashal bicolon.

68:14 is only a quasi-tricolon; v. 14a has no real connection whatever, neither with v. 13 nor with v. 14b ,c. It is in all probability but a marginal quotation from Jud. 5:16. See my *Der Achtundsechzigste Psalm*, p. 35.

A secondary addition is also **68:17c** with its «Yahweh» within this «elohistic» psalm. See *op.cit.* p. 41.

For any theory of sporadic tricola in bicolic poems **68:19** is quite useless. V. 19c — too long for any known type of cola — makes no sense at all. Cpr. *op.cit.* p. 41.

78:21,31,71. The metre of this psalm consists of regular Mashal bicola; in v. 55c,d a *kol-* before *šibte* or a *'ammo* behind *yiśrâ'el*, or both, have fallen out. — The apparent tricola vv. 21, 31, 71 seem, all of them, to be due to secondary glosses (and/or variants). V. 21c is in all probability a text-variant, or a secondary false parallel colon. Between the perfect thought rhymes v. 30a,b and 31b,c, v. 31a makes the strong impression of a secondary addition, taken from Nu. 11:33; the clause is quite unnecessary; the whole passage vv. 23—31 describes the planned result of the wrath of Yahweh, as is already said in v. 21. V. 31a is an explanatory addition.

86:14c. On the metrical structure of this psalm see above p. 43. Vv. 7, 14—15 call for Yahweh's help and motivate the prayer by pointing to the tyrant enemies who try to kill the worshipper. In *this* connection the words «they do not set thee before them» («they care nothing for thee», Moffatt) are at least unnecessary. In view of the metre of the psalm they may be considered as a gloss after 54:5.

122:5 an adherent of Sievers's metrical system might take as a two-beat tricolon although the 3rd «colon» *kis'ot lebet dâwid*, even by a Sieversian, ought to be scanned as a 3-beat verse. But in all probability *lemišpâṭ* is a gloss out of an eschatological interpretation of the psalm — in itself it has no eschatological traits. Then the verse consists of a normal Qinah bicolon of the repetitive type.

d) As we have seen above, § 4, there certainly are cases where either other text-witnesses or exegetical reasons or both indicate that a colon or more has been lost in TM. Even in these cases the conclusions have often been corroborated by the metre. The possibility exists that the same may have happened in other cases as well, and that we are not unjustified in using even the metre as an indication, *that a colon has been lost*, and that apparent tricola only are due to such a textual corruption.

5:9 is such an apparent tricolon. As the psalm is written in Qinah metre, two and two Qinah stichs making a stanza respectively, we may well assume that in v. 9b the shorter second colon, parall. *lema‘an śorerây*, has been lost.

A similar lacuna may be supposed in **6:7**, the 1st colon of which seems very abrupt. Something like *yhwh, we'en menuḥâ me'ænqâti* should fit the context and parallelism and make the bicolon full.

An apparent tricolon is **7:6**, the division of the lines, however, in BHK is wrong, v. 6b and 6c are parallel (make a thought rhyme) and ought to have been printed on the same line. The metre of the psalm is, as we have seen, (p. 23), the Mashal, arranged in accordance with the «basic stanza». Then we should expect two bicola in v. 6 as well. Now both metre and parallelism seem to demand that v. 6b begins with *weyirdom*, but then *weyaśśeg* has no object. So we may suppose that something like *'oti çorer* has been lost behind *weyaśśeg*.

On Ps. **11** see above p. 23. If we are right in finding there 5 «basic stanzas», we expect *v. 6* to consist of 2 bicola, the first of which is to be connected with v. 5, the second with v. 7, Now 6a is obviously too long for a single colon; *'eš wegofrit*, however, is too short to make one. Perhaps we may supplement a *yhwh* after *yamṭir*, let the caesura fall before *påhim*, and put a *we* before *'eš*. Then the second bicolon begins with *weruᵃh*, before this word, however, a word seems to be missing, e.g. *sufå*. This emendation may at least be preferred to the deletion of *wĕgofrit*, as proposed by BHK.

As I have shown in details in my article «Zum Psalm 16,2—4», *Theologische Literaturzeitung* 1957, Nr. 9, col. 649 ff, we have both a wrong verse division and a mutilated text in **16:2—4**. Vv. 1 and 2a belong together as parallel cola of a bicolon (pronounce *'åmarti*, delete *'ådonåy*, cpr. BHK). *bal-ʿålækå* makes no sense connected with v. 2; even the metre shows that it must be connected with v. 3. But even then, vv. 3—4 do not make sense. Only so much is certain, that the worshipper here abjures, as the negative correspondent to v. 1—2, every connection with other powers than Yahweh. For *haq-qedošim*, without any further determination, in O.T. always mean superhuman beings[1] and *addirim* is here a synonym of *qedošim*, with the same meaning; see 1 Sam. 4:6; Sir. 50:16; Ps. 78:25. But then *kol-ḥæfçi-båm* says just the opposite of what must be said here; there can be no doubt that we must read *bal-ḥæfçi båm*, and a similar expression must be conjectured instead of the meaningless words *bal-ʿålækå*. As v. 3a now speaks of «the *qĕdošim* on the earth», both the logic of the thought and the parallelism demand that the *'addirim* are the other category of «saints» and «powers», at whose sacrifices (v. 4) the worshipper confesses not to have taken part, nor does he want to have anything to do with them. On the basis of these exegetical considerations I propose the following text:

$$³beliyyaʿal kol-qĕdošim bå'åræç$$
$$weʾaddire haššåmayim bal-ḥæfçi båm;$$
$$yarbu ʿaççebotåm 'aharehæm miharu.$$

The last colon of v. 4a is lost; it may have had a wording like this:

$$kåšelu 'ašær låhæm råçu.$$

An apparent tricolon at the end of the psalm is also **16:11**. The Massoretic interpunction, however, and the division of the printed lines in BHK are wrong; obviously 11b and 11c belong

---

[1] S. also M. Noth in the *Mowinckel-Festskrift*, Oslo 1955, pp. 146ff.

closer to each other and make a regular thought rhyme (parallelism), containing a new thought element; 11a is an isolated single colon. This lack of parallelism is strange in a psalm where the thought rhyme plays a great rôle. As, however, the text of Ps. 16 admittedly is very bad, I see no difficulty in assuming that a colon, parall. 11a has been lost.

23:4b (from *ki'attá*) seems to be a tripartite verse. The metre of the psalm i Qinah, the verse division in TM is, however, incorrect; v. 2a must be connected with v. 1, and 2 b with 3a (see BHK), thus making the first basic stanza. The second stanza consists of vv. 3b, 4a (to *rá'* incl., where Atnach); the fourth of v. 5, the sixth of v. 6. There is, then, all reason to think that v. 4b originally has made a whole stanza, the third. Now *šibṭeká* etc. make a correct Qinah verse. *ki 'attá 'immádi* build, however, only the half of a Qinah verse. The supposition seems alloved that some words have been lost. The line may originally have run:

ki 'attá [yhwh] 'immádi / ['attá maḥasi].

In all probability some words have been lost in **28:5b**, where we may supplement something like *welo' yibnehæm*. Qinah metre, 2 such verses to a stanza.

31:24 is no tricolon; v. 24c is a new «verse-line» of its own. But no single colon either; it contains more than the 4 (or 3) regular pedes of a colon. The psalm is written in Qinah metrum; it is not necessary here to deal with the apparent irregularities in vv. 10, 18, 19. V. 24c, however, is a little too short for a regular Qinah; a word or two may have been lost. At all events, vv. 24—25 make a stanza consisting of 3 (Qinah) bicola, and just of such stanzas, the whole psalm is built, see above pp. 29ff.

32:2b BHK proposes to delete. I prefer to think that the short membrum has been lost. Qinah metre, stanzas to 3 Qinah bicola each, except in vv. 8—9 (four bicola).

As in 32, the metrical structure in **36** is regular stanzas each consisting of three Qinah bicola. In *v. 5a*, however, the shorter link of the Qinah is missing. I think it may be filled up after Mi. 2:1 *be'or habboqær ya^{ea}śehá*.

In **39** too, the metre is the Qinah; two bicola make a stanza. Even *v. 13* consists — against the division of the lines in BHK — of two Qinoth; the shorter part of v. 13b, however, has been lost.

48:9 has from the viewpoint of quantity, material enough for the 2 Qinah bicola, which the metre and the strophic structure demand. But no regular metre is found in TM, and within the «Elohimpsalter» *be'ir yhwh çĕbâ'ot* is only a variant of *be'ir 'ælohenu*. Then v. 9b lacks the shorter colon. Suppl. something like *bal timmoṭ* (*le'olâm*), cp. 46:6; these words have been ousted by the doublet *b.y.ç.*, which, then, indirectly testifies to the lost words.

In **52:3—4** the Massoretic verse division is wrong. As the metre, Qinah, shows, *kol-hay-yom* v. 3 must be connected with v. 4; the rest of v. 3 is a correct Qinah. (Read *'æl-ḥasid*, BHK). In v. 4 the interpunction is wrong; *lešonekâ* must be connected with the following word, thus making a correct Qinah. See BHK. Then in all probability vv. 3b—4a, too, originally have made a Qinah verse; as BHK suggests, some words are missing after 4b, once making the Qinah full; we may supplement *ta'ᵃśæ mezimmâ* or the like.
52:7 now looks like a Mashal tricolon. But *yittâçĕkâ lânæçaḥ* comes too early; it must be the last act, or the last result of God's destroying the tyrant; when these words are replaced at the end of the verse, we have 2 regular Qinah verses even here. In so fare, v. 7 belongs in § 7a. — **52:11** finally is now a 4-beat colon and a Qinah; but in v. a at least an object to *'ᵃśitâ* is lacking. *šimekâ* in v. b gives reason to the supposition that the name really has been mentioned in the preceding line. A text like this:

'odekâ yhwh le'olâm | ki 'ᵃśitâ ḥæsæd 'immi

should make the Qinah full and the meaning quite clear. Read *wa'aḥawwæ* for *wa'aqawwæ*.

55:24 seems to contain 1 bicolon and 1 single colon — no real tricolon — making the end of this psalm of lamentation. After the lamentation with its motivations of the prayer («Gebetserhörungs-motive») in vv. 2—22 the answer follows in v. 23 through the mouth of the priest with the promise of Yahweh's gracious help. The usual rules of composition[1] demand that this oracle be followed by the worshipper's expression of his confidence and his thanks, sometimes in the form of an anticipated thanksgiving, as if the salvation already had become full reality; here often the vows are given or mentioned; sometimes also a repeated short prayer is included: might God's intercession come soon! — Of these elements our v. 24 only contains the repeated prayer in v. a, with an expression of the confidence that wicked «bloody and deceitful men» never will live out half their days, v.b. V. c begins, in the form of a nominal clause, by expressing the worshipper's confidence: «But I trust in thee». One cannot help feeling that the psalm ends very abruptly, and that here something is lacking; what is the definite content of his confidence in this specific situation? After the antithetically sounding «But I» we expect to hear what he expects for himself, as opposite to the expected fall of his enemies. And what about the thanksgiving and the vows? — Now G has at least 1 word more: a «Yahweh» after *bekå*, which indicates that the last line or lines of the psalm have been lost. In this connection, it is not unimportant that also in v. 20 at least 1 bicolon seems to have been lost; *'ašær* has no clear·reference, and, opposite the other stanzas of the psalm, which consist of 2 bicola each, vv. 20—21 contain 3, either 1 too much or 1 too little. — So we have very good reasons for the opinion that v. 24c is no single colon, but only the rest of a bicolon.

62:12—13 apparently are two tricolic verses, whereas the main corpus of the psalm is written in Qinah metre (see above p. 32). That is clearly the reason why BHK connects 12b with 13a, taking these elements as one Qinah bicolon. That does not, however, suffice; v. 12b cannot be scanned as a longer, 4-beat part of a Qinah, but only as 3 beats at most; moreover, *ʿoz* and *ḥæsæd* are not the right synonyms for a thought rhyme. TM has felt that v. 13a sounds as a new beginning; the right synonym to *ḥæsæd* is however, *'æmunå* (or *'æmæt*), cpr. 40:12; 61:8. Some words seem to have been lost between v. 12 and v. 13, among these also a synonym

---

[1] S. Gunkel-Begrich, *Einleitung in die Psalmen*, Göttingen 1933, pp. 243ff; Mowinckel, *Offersang og Sangoffer*, pp. 194ff, 231ff.

of ʿoz. What the original wording of v. 12b may have been, is impossible to tell; v. 13a may have had something like this:

uleká yhwh ḥæsæd | uleká ʾæmæt.

In **63:12** something seems to have been lost at the end of the psalm. 2 and 2 Mashal bicola build a stanza respectively. With v. 12c the psalm scarcely can have ended; every reader feels that the expression of the worshipper's confidence at the end of the psalm cannot have been content with the mentioning of the fall of the enemies only; it must have had its positive side as well. The antithetic sentence «But I . . .» expressing the worshipper's confidence in his own salvation and everlasting security in Yahweh's shelter, is missing. At least 3 cola seem to have been lost.

Another possibility is, however, that v. 12c is but an additional gloss, underlining unnecessarily why the king and the faithful shall rejoice. For both the negative and the positive side of the salvation as reason for rejoicing are already mentioned in vv. 11, 12a, b. — If this be the case, 63:12 belongs in § 8c.

68:3 is apparently a tricolon. V. 3c, however, is too long for a regular 4-beat colon, especially when we realize that the plus in G, *ken*, certainly is original. Then we have every reason to believe that more than *ken* has been lost, and that v. 3c, too, originally was a bicolon. One might suppose *mippene ʾælohim* (originally: *yhwh*) *mippene ʾælohenu*; some copyist has over-seen the two lost words because of the great similarity with the two preceding ones.

71. Above p. 28 we have dealt with *v. 18*. The metre of this psalm is mostly Qinah, in other cases, e.g. vv. 9—12, Mashal. This irregularity may be due to the fact that the psalm is very little original but is mostly patched together of conventional phrases; especially the relationship to Ps. 31 is obvious. As a rule, however, two and two bicola make a stanza, e.g. vv. 5—6a, 8—9, 10—11, 12—13, 14—15a, 17—18a, 18b—19a, 19b—20a, 20b—21, 22, 24. This makes it very probable that vv. 1—3 must be reconstructed in cooperation with a reconstruction of 31:1—3 — in both cases it is e.g. obvious, that a new bicolon must begin with v. 2b and that vv. 1—3 originally have had either 3 or 5 bicola; v. 3c is strophi-

cally to be connected with v. 4. The details are of no importance
for our investigation; the reconstructed text of vv. 1—4a, therefore,
may be given without further commentary:

¹*bekå yhwh hasiti | ʾal ʾebošå leʿolåm*
²*beçidqatekå taççileni | palleteni wehošiʿeni*
hatte ʾelay ʾoznekå | meherå wehaççileni
³*haye li leçur måʿoz | lebet meçudåti.*
ki salʿi umeçudåti ʾattå | meçurat yešuʿåti
⁴ʾ*ælohay palleteni miyyad råšåʿ | mikkaf meʿawwel wehomeç.*

The *vv. 6, 13, 15 and 23* demand a closer consideration.

V. 13 makes no real difficulty. The supernumerary words
mĕbaqqĕše råʿåti are simply an explanatory gloss taken over from
v. 24; they add nothing to *šoṭene nafši*.

V. 15 is an apparent tricolon. It is, however, quite obvious
that something is missing behind *seforot*. AV translates: «I do not
know the numbers (thereof)», i.e. of «thy *çedåqå*, a «number», however,
presupposes a plural word, to which to refer. *sfrwt* must here have
the meaning of a verb in inf. = *lisefor*, and as object something
like *niflåʾotækå ugedolotækå* must be supplemented.

It is likewise obvious that a verb is missing in *v. 23c*. V. a,b
forms a correct Qinah: «my eyes shall greatly rejoice/ when I sing
unto thee», and then a new Qinah: «my soul, which thou hast
redeemed/ . . .» What about the soul? Of course, something like
tåširå lehasdækå must be supplemented.

This all being so, I feel no doubt that behind *v. 6c* a colon,
whether it be a mashal colon or a shorter second Qinah colon, has
been lost.

Ps. 72 is built up of regular stanzas, two Qinah bicola to a
stanza. This verdict, however, presupposes that v. 3 has to be
replaced after v. 7. Vv. 2 and 4 are speaking of the King's *çædæq*
and *mišpåṭ*, and that means here clearly his moral and judicial
qualities as a just king. V. 7 likewise speaks of the *çædæq* (BHK)
and *šålom*, that his rule will bring; but the words here just as
clearly mean the luck and good fortune and welfare of his rule.

Šålom and *çedåqå* obviously have this last meaning in v. 3 as
well; the verse deals with such *šålom* and *çedåqå* as «the mountains

and the hills» shall bring forth. V. 3 thus evidently is to be connected with v. 7. The displacing in TM is due to a later misunderstanding of the key words, that has resulted in a mis-remembering at the stage of oral tradition. In so fare a case sub § 7a.

This being so, there is every reason to believe that a first membrum of a Qinah has been lost in front of v. *4c*. BHK proposes to delete the words *widakke ʿošeq*, as other commentators have done. I think we more often have to assume that some words have fallen out rather than that some have been wrongly added.

The former is obviously the case in **74:2**. *naḥălåtekå* here is the same as *ʿadåtekå*, but then *har çiyyon* etc. logically is no good apposition to those words. BHK proposes to delete v. 2b; but that would not make things better; to *ʿadåtekå* v. 2c *har çiyyon* etc. is a still more inappropriate apposition. — In fact, something is missing to which *har çiyyon* can refer. That means: a colon before *har ç.* has been lost, something like *ʾal tiškaḥ miqdåš konenu yådækå*. The strophic structure of the psalm then appears quite clear: two and two Mashal bicola make a stanza, respectively vv. 1—2a,b (re-constructed), 2c—3, 4—5, 6—7 etc. In v. 17 a *kol-leʾummim* must be supplemented according to the parallelism.

The case in **84:4** is an analoguos one. The words *ʾæt mizbe-ḥotækå* etc. are formally a Qinah verse, as are the other clear verses of this psalm. (On vv. 7,11 see below). Syntactically *ʾæt mizbeḥotækå* etc. are the continuation of the preceding clause, apparently an explicative apposition to *bayit* and *qen*. So one might think that the relative clause *ʾašær šattå ʾæfroḥæhå* be an explanatory, but quite unnecessary gloss; the birds normally do not use their nest for anything else than as a place where to lay their *ʾæfroᵃh*. But logically the bicola of this psalm belong together two and two (the «basic stanza»): vv. 2—3a, 3b—4a, 5—6, 7, 9b—10, 11, 12 (v. 13 seems to be a final liturgical refrain, see below § 9b). Then we must suppose that even the rest of v. 4 once has made such a short stanza, and that the short membrum of a Qinah has been lost behind *ʾæfroḥæhå*. That the text of this psalm is incomplete, we see in v. 7b too, where the necessary direct object to *yaʿṭæ* is missing; probably *ʾæt-midbår* must be supplemented (vok. *berekot*); or v. 7b

may be a comparison, read *yāʿaṭehu kammorœ hammidbår*. Even in
v. 11 a word is missing after *meʾælæf*, obviously *båḥarti* must be
corrected in *beḥadere*, and *hon* supplemented; read *ʾašær* for *ræšaʿ*.
In **84:8** too, the shorter colon of the Qinah seems to have fallen
out. If our observations on the metre and the strophic structure
are correct, the new section of the psalm must begin not with v.
10, as TM seems to think, but with v. 9; *šimʿå tẹfillåti, haʾᵃzinå/*
ʾælohe yaʿᵃqob is a correct Qinah, 9b—10 make a regular stanza.
Accordingly the first 3 words in v. 9 must be connected with v. 8,
which then continues only 3 cola instead of the expected 4; the lost
shorter colon has had its place after v. 8a.

The text then runs like this:
> [8]*yeleku meḥayl ʾæl ḥayl* / [. . . . .]
> *yirʾu ʾel ʾælohim beçiyyon* /[9] *yhwh ʾælohe çẹbåʾot.*
> *šimʿå tẹfillåti haʾᵃzinå* / *ʾælohe yaʿᵃqob* etc.

Apparently **104:24—25** consist of 2 tricola. But one becomes
puzzled observing that v. 25a is much too long for a normal colon;
it cannot be scanned otherwise than as a 3 + 3 or perhaps a 3 + 2
verse.

Bickel and Duhm have seen that with a little rearrangement
of the verse order the psalm is built up of regular stanzas, 5 Mashal
bicola to the stanza; one only needs to put v. 16 before and v. 17
behind v. 12. In my opinion they are quite right. Then vv. 24—26
build one stanza. Instead of 10 cola they now seem to consist of
only 8; but as we just have seen, v. 25a certainly has material for
more than 1 colon. The BHK print is misleading, for v. 25b and c
are the right parallel lines and build the thought rhyme, and should
therefore have been printed on the same line. In v. 25a we only
need to supplement one word to have a normal bicolon; read
hayyåm haggådol/ råb ureḥåb etc. Then only a parallel to v. 24c is
missing. I have no hezitation in adding something like *wetebel niflåʾotækå.*

In *v. 29*, too, 1 colon is missing. BHK proposes to delete v. c,
but even here, not deleting, but filling up, is the right solution.
The opposition *ruᵘḥ* — *ʿåfår* shows that v. b and c are two parallel

cola; the lost colon must have had its place behind v. a. Something like *weḥabbe meḥæm yo'bedun* must be supplemented.

Logically **106:43c** has its natural place before v. a,b; as to the content, vv. 43a and 44 belong together. The old displacement has, however, had as its result, that the original parallel colon to v. 43c has been lost. Even here BHK proposes to solve the problem by deleting v. 43c. But the regular stanza structure (two bicola a stanza) shows that we have to fill up, and not to delete.

That **115:7** must be filled up from the parallel 135:17, is at least very probable.

On pp. 71 and 67 above we have dealt with Ps. 116:3 and 116:16; here some remarks on **116:8**. But first a few words about the metrical structure. Most of the bicola are clear Qinah verses. V. 3c is a variant of 3a,b; v. 16 once, in all probability, was a complete Qinah. — Now it is clear that v. 14 is nothing but a dittography of v. 18 and, rightly, is lacking in several G-mss. But then it is obvious that the psalm is built up of regular stanzas, two Qinah verses making a stanza. Vv. 5—6 certainly are one, vv. 10—11 another, opening a new section of the poem. — Then the first part of v. 8 must belong together with v. 7, and the last part with v. 9. But v. 8 now consists only of 3 cola instead of 4. A short colon + a new verb, e.g. *hošǎ'tā*, have been lost after *mimmåwæt*.

In **118**, too, the single stanzas consist of 2 bicola each; the only exception is vv. 5—7, where vv. 6 and 7 may be variants. A new section and a new liturgical scene start with v. 27, another separate section is vv. 28—29, a little thanksgivings psalm summing up the content of the whole series of scenes to which the psalm is the song text. Accordingly vv. 27 and 28—29 must be considered as two separate stanzas. — But *v. 27* only consists of 1½ bicolon instead of 2. To speak here of a tricolon (Albright) makes no sense; the two parts of the verse are relatively independent of each other; v. 27a a word of praise, v. 27b,c a call to the participants of the procession to form a connected rank, touching each other and the altar, with their festal green branches. So there is some reason to believe that some words have been lost in v. 27a, and that this apparent single colon once was a full bicolon. See, however, below § 10.

128 consists of 4 stanzas, 2 Qinah verses to a stanza; v. 5b,c goes together with v. 6; only *v. 5a* is no full bicolon, neither a Qinah nor a Mashal; 1 colon is missing. I think we are justified supplementing *'ośe śâmayim wâʾâræç*, in accordance with 124:8; 134:3.

133 consists of 3 stanzas of the same type; v. 2a,b (read: *kizeqan*) goes together with v. 1, and v. 2c,d with v. 3a,b (read: *harere ʿiyyon*). The rest of *v. 3* builds the last stanza, beginning with *ki* and giving the motivation of the preceding verses. We expect to find 2 Qinah verses (4 cola) here as in the other stanzas, but TM has only 3 cola. In all probability the longer part of the last Qinah, something like *weśâm yitten haś-śâlom*, has been lost before *hayyim* etc.

141:5 has 3 cola, but is no real tricolon. The division of the lines in BHK is scarcely correct; v. 5c seems to be the parallel colon to 5b, in antithetical parallelism: I do not take part in the festal meals of the wicked (read *râśâ*, G, S), on the contrary *(ki)*, «I am always praying (read: *'odi tefillâti*) for his calamities», i.e. I pray that the just revenge may fall upon him. The abjuration of every sort of fellowship with the wicked starts already in v. 4c, a verb must be supplemented, probably *lo' 'okel*, cpr. 101:5 G, S. V. 4c,d must then be connected with v. 5a. Here, however, the text is altogether unclear: «May a just one (or: The Just One, but should we not then expect *haççaddiq?*) suit me, loyalty, and may he reprove me». The text is certainly corrupt and incomplete, and gives no basis for the supposition of a tricolon; on the contrary, there is every reason to think that v. 5a has been a bicolon, as are all the other stichs of this psalm.

If so, we shall have 6 regular «basic stanzas» vv. 1—2; 3—4b; 4c—5a; 5b—6; 7—8; 9—10.

142 is written in clear cut Qinah metre. Three Qinoth make a stanza, four stanzas: vv. 2—4a; 4b—5; 6—7a; 7b—8. The only exception is *v. 6b*, where the shorter second colon is missing. Personally, I feel quite convinced that a clause, parall. 6aβ, has been lost. After 141:8 I propose: *bekâ yhwh hâsiti*.

148:13—14 are in TM treated as two tricola. BHK takes v. 14a as the parallel colon to v. 13c, thus making three bicola out of these verses. Here BHK is wrong; v. 13 is the general call on all beings of the whole universe to praise Him whose name alone is exalted and whose glory is above both earth and heaven; v. 14 speaks of what he has done for Israel and what is the special reason for his people to give him praise. TM's division of the transmitted text is correct. V. 14 introduces a new thought not only as compared with v. 13, but also as compared with the whole psalm. Now we see that the whole psalm from v. 1 to v. 12 is built up of clear cut and distinct stanzas, 2 bicola to the stanza: vv. 1—2; 3—4; 5—6; 7—8; 9—10; 11—12. We should then expect that if it were the poet's intention to end the peoem with 2 tricola, even this verse pair would make a consistent stanza, i.e. that they logically should hang together and make a unit; but, as we have seen, v. 14 introduces a completely new thought. And I think that most readers, acquainted with the formal rules of Hebrew poetry, expect that both v. 13c and v. 14a should be rounded off by a parallel colon respectively. The strophic regularity of the psalm seems to justify the expectation that both v. 13 and v. 14 are intended to make a «basic stanza» respectively. — That means: there are both formal and logical reasons to believe that 2 cola have been lost between vv. 13 and 14. The wording of the lost cola can only be guessed; to me it seems a reasonable guess to supplement v. 13c after 57:6, and v. 14a after 29:11 (cpr. 89:18, and 92:11), reading

> hodo ʿal ʾæræç wešåmayim
> [ukebodo ʿal kol-tebel]
> weyårem (G, S, Hie) qæræn leʿammo
> [ycbarek yiśråʾel beʿoz].

150, a hymn of praise, formally consisting of the normal «introitus» only, the call to praise, seems to have been built up of 3 normal stanzas: vv. 1—2: where and why Yahweh should be praised, vv. 3—4: by which means, the musical instruments of the choir, vv. 5—6: continuation and final: by whom. — When now vv. 5—6 consists of 3 cola only, the 3rd of which is no real parallel to the 2 former, but brings in a new thought element («by whom»), we expect that even this thought would be expressed by 2 parallel clauses, something like *kol-ḥay yehallelu yâh*. A colon at the end of the psalm seems to have been lost.

9.

As we have seen above in § 2, we have to distinguish between a real tricolon and an *isolated single colon* among regular bicola.

How shall we have to judge about the latter phenomenon?

Many apparent single colon have in the above investigation proved to be due to textual corruption that can be remedied by the ordinary means of textual criticism, to displacement, to lacunae in the text, to textual doublets and variants, to secondary elements as glosses and the like. That this is true in prophetic metrical texts as well, I have demonstrated on a series of samples in *ZATW* 68, pp. 104ff.

But there are cases where this explanation does not seem to hold good.

a) First we have a little group where a definite and special part of the psalm is introduced by an *introductory formula extra metrum*.

This we have in **2:7a**, where the King quotes the installation oracle from Yahweh and introduces it by the introductory formula: «I will declare the proclamation (or decree) of Yahweh». See above p. 47.

The same *may* be the case with the introductory formula in **110:1**. Here, however, it is possible that the formula forms part of the metrical structure, as does in all probability, the introduction in v. 4a.

81:6c has nothing to do with vv. 2—6b, with which TM has connected it. The line is the formula by which the cult prophet introduces his oracle in vv. 7—17 as an inspiration from a supernatural voice. As most usual in prophetic style the introductory formula stands extra metrum (Mashal bicola, 2 to each stanza). See above p. 37f.

As we have seen above, p. 64, **66:16** may have been an introductory formula outside the strophic structure of the psalm.

b) In other cases, we have to do with *text-elements that do not belong to the psalm-text proper* but must be considered whether it be as liturgical formulae spoken in connection with the performance of the psalm, or as some sort of refrain or response, either at the end of an important stanza or section of the psalm, or at the end of the whole psalm, or to be repeated after each stanza, or the like.

That such elements are found in the transmitted psalm-texts, is but to be expected, just because we have to do with liturgical texts, used at the festal cultus in the temple and sung by the choir of the singers, in some cases certainly antiphonically by two choirs. The «Hallelujah» at the end — and/or beginning — of many psalms certainly is to be considered in this way. We have in other words here to do with *refrains* or the like that do not necessarily belong within the metrical scheme of the psalm in question.

Among the transmitted psalms there certainly are some where we find such extra metrical refrains.

A rather certain case of this sort we have in **103:22**, where v. c takes up again the introitus in vv. 1a, 2a: «Bless Yahweh, O my soul!» As an organic part of the last three verses: the call to the whole universe to «bless» Yahweh, a repeated call to «my soul» should sound rather faint. Quite another impression is made, however, when we imagine it as repeated by the choir after every bicolon or every stanza, thus holding fast and stressing the intention and the emotion of the psalm expressed already in the first lines. In this case the refrain plays the same rôle as the «Hallelujah» at the end of Pss. 113ff, which certainly does not belong to the metrical psalm-text proper.

Just the same is to be said about **104:35c**. On the strophic division of the psalm see above p. 83.

In a similar way we have to judge **2:12c**. The «psalm» as a whole is a solemn «proclamation» of the new King at the cultic celebration of his anointment and coronation, with a warning against the vassals' vain plans of insurrection. The last stanza vv. 10—12 repeats this warning expressis verbis: «be wise and take warning, serve Yahweh and submit to him» etc. Included in this warning is no doubt the submission to Yahweh's viceroy, his anointed King on Zion. It must be admitted that an exclamation of confidence in

Yahweh has no special logical connection with this theme; the context does not speak of confidence, but of submission and service out of fear. On the other hand, a fixed formula as v. 12c *can* be added to nearly every religious context, let alone the logical connection. And as a liturgical «rounding off» the formula here is best explained.

This seems very probable also from another consideration. The psalm has in later Jewish cults no coubt been interpreted as «Messianic»; the reference to the earthly king has been forgotten and the psalm understood as referring to the coming Messiah and as a glorification of the Lord who in due time will let him come; Yahweh, not the King has become the central theme of the psalm. And, in fact, it seems to me very probable that the original wording in vv. 11—12 has not been about submission and «worship» (*ʿåbad*) of Yahweh, but submission under the King on Zion and «service» (*åbad*) as his slaves. If so, the exclamation in v. 12c and the benediction of «all who trust in him», i.e. Yahweh, is a consequence of this re-interpretation and of the cultic use of the psalm in this new light.

As mentioned above p. 69, **20:6c** may be taken as a sort of refrain, making no part of the metrical structure of the psalm itself.[1]

c) Besides the short refrains there may have been cases where the recitation of the psalm had to be interrupted by *liturgical formulae* to be spoken in connection with the performance. The border between these two categories fluctuates.

125:5 is no real tricolon; v. c *šålom ʿal yiśråʾel* is a new thought in relation to the preceding verses. These contain, against the

---

[1] Agreeing with Bertholet (in Kautzsch, *Die Heilige Schrift des A.T.*, 4th Ed., Tübingen 1923), Gunkel thinks he has found a «stylistic rule» according to which a psalm often ends with a single colon, even psalms with regular stanzas (*Die Psalmen*, p. 12). Our investigation has shown that of all his examples only some 5 remain, and here we have to do with liturgical formulae, that neither belong to the psalm text proper, nor to the metrical formation of the psalm in question. All the other irregularities postulated by Gunkel, have found their explanation in our investigation (3:8; 7:6;12:6; 13:6; 14:7; 16:11; 18: 49, 51; 19:7; 27:6; 31:24; 55:24; 69:37 (read: 69:36); 72:15,17; 79:13; 94:23; 99:5,9; 100:5; 103:22; 104:35; 106:5; 129: 8; 133:3; 138:8; 143:12).

background of the expression of the confidence v. 1—3, a prayer about fortune for the «just» i.e. Israel, and destruction for the wicked and the «evil-doers», v. 4—5a,b; v. 5c, however, is a word of blessing, an answer to the prayer. In the liturgy we may assume that it was spoken by the priest(s) as the answer to the prayer-psalm of the choir. — Accordingly it does not belong to the metrical structure of the psalm itself (3 stanzas, 2 Qinah bicola to a stanza), but stands outside it.

We have an indisputable liturgical formula in **129:8c**. This line can, of course, not be the continuation of the greeting formula from the every-day language in v. 8b, spoken by those «which go by»; 8c is a priestly formula of blessing, spoken within the frame of the ritual, cpr. 118:26; Dtn. 10:8. It does not belong to the psalm-text proper and its metrical structure, but must be interpreted as the blessing formula with which the priest answers the prayer of the psalm. — The metrical observations corroborate this interpretation. The psalm is written in Qinah metre; without v. 8c it quite clearly is built up of 2 regular stanzas, 4 bicola to each, vv. 1—4; 5—8b.

A part of the liturgy and no part of the psalm itself (a tricolon) we also may have in **3:8a**. The psalm is a «psalm of protection», the only theme of which is the confidence of the worshipper: Yahweh will certainly not disappoint his servant, who so exclusively sets all his hope on Him. — Very strange is here indeed the short cry of prayer («Gebetsruf») in v. 8a «Arise, O Yahweh, save me, O my God!» — isolated as it stands among mere expressions of confidence; with its quite different content, it makes no real «tricolon» together with v. 8b,c. — I should like to make the suggestion, that this sentence does not belong to the psalm itself and its metrical scheme, but is the prayer that, at the recitation of the psalm in the cult, should be cried by the chorus as a sort of refrain after every «stanza» of the psalm, that means, after every two bicola. That the psalm has to be divided in such «basic stanzas», is in this case expressly indicated by the «selah» vv. 3, 5, 9. But why then, one may ask, not also behind v. 7? That is just the point of departure of my above suggestion. V. 8a is just what was to be cried at the moments indicated by the «*selah*». In my opinion Eerdmans (*The Hebrew Book of Psalms*, Leiden 1947, pp. 80ff) is quite right in taking *selah* as «to bow», indicating the places in the recitation of the psalm where the congregation had to bow down, to fall to the earth. That on these occasions something was said, is in my opinion demonstrated by the massoretic vocalization of the word, which according to the old versions obviously means *næçah* «for ever». The cry of prayer or homage that was declaimed on those occasions, may have been different, according to the nature of the cult act and the content of the psalm; it may sometimes have been «Hallelujah», very often «For ever», to stress the words of the prayer or homage. In the case of Ps. 3, it can have been v. 8a. This verse represents the content of the «selah», marked after the other «stanzas». These, then, *in this case* mean: to bow down and cry: «Arise, Yahweh, and save me, my God!» Because the words themselves were put after v. 7, no «selah» was necessary here.

10.

We have, however, also to reckon with the probability that such liturgical formulae have been taken up in the tenor of the psalm by the poet himself, and that this may have caused some irregularity in the metrical structure used elsewhere in the poem concerned. The well-known solemn formula, e.g. a blessing formula, then is thought to be of such a material weight that it even might, both poetically and metrically have got the weight of a longer line. The lack of length may have been counterbalanced by a pause, or a repetition, or by its being sung by a solo voice or by another choir.

118:27 may represent one of these cases, s. above pp. 84f. V. 27a at least makes the impression of being a fixed liturgical formula, like e.g. Ex 15:2a,b cpr. Isa. 12:2a,c,d; for the verb *he'ir* in such a connection may be referred to Nu. 6:25 — by the way, in a tripartite liturgical formula.

Another instance, where this possibility may be taken into consideration, is **22:27c**. Compared with 69:33 this sentence seems to have been a fixed formula through which the worshipper, offering his thanks-offering, invited the guests to come and take part in the sacrificial meal and thus «strengthen their hearts» and «live».

A more or less fixed formulation may be the reason why the answer to the question about the conditions of entering the holy place, **24:4** consists of three links. There are, however, other possibilities. Seen in the light of Ps. 15, 24:4 has the character of an enumeration of certain links of a well-known longer chain of commandments, the «decalogical tradition», the full form of which we have in Ps. 15.[1] In the liturgy reflected in Ps. 24, the answer may have been longer, the scribe giving only the first lines of a longer formula. — Contrariwise, v. 4c may be a later addition, motivated by a desire of a tripartite answer. But note that even without v. c, the bicolon 4a,b just gives three conditions: cleanness of the hands, purity of the heart, and avoidance of all connection with the powers of *šā'w*, the «lie». Without v. 4c the whole psalm would be built up of regular stanzas, each of them consisting of two «long verses», bicola (vv. 1—6) and tricola (vv. 7—10).

There is another case where an isolated tricolon may be due to the fact that the poet here gives an enumeration from a well-known list, namely **68:28**, where the representatives of the Is-raelitic tribes are mentioned. Here we have a tricolon within a stanza where, according to the strophic structure of the psalm, we should expect bicola only (4 in number, see above p. 41f). As the representatives of the festal procession are here by way of example mentioned: «Benjamin, the youngest, their ruler, the princes of Judah, their leader(?), the princes of Zebulun, the princes of Naphtali». — There is every reason to believe that the tribes re-presented in the procession by their chieftains («princes») are real political entities. In *«Der achtundsechzigste Psalm»* pp. 53ff I have discussed the problem as follows: The order of the tribes in the procession must express a political reality; the tribe that marches at the front must be the «royal» tribe. But here we have two «royal» tribes: Benjamin «their (i.e. the other tribes) ruler (*rodem*)» and «Judah *rigmâtâm*», although the exact meaning of this word is uncertain, it in all probability means something like «leader», «ruler» Now there never was a time in the history of Israel where Benjamin *and* Judah had the leadership, the hegemony. Therefore, one of

---

[1] See *Offersang og Sangoffer* pp. 329ff.

these two tribes must later have been interpolated in the text. No one would, however, be interested in putting Benjamin into the text at a time when this tribe did not have any political importance, not to say further existence. Thus we are led to believe that the psalm was made at a time when Benjamin was the royal tribe, the time of Saul (or Ishba῾al). Judah has been intercalated at a time when this tribe had become the «royal» one, and the psalm used on festal occasions at the Davidic temple of Jerusalem.

Today I realize that this argument does not hold good. There is another possibility, at which I had hinted *op.cit.* p. 53, and which I now think is much more probable. If the psalm were Saulidic and later remodelled for the Davidic-Salomonic temple, why did they not simply put Judah instead of Benjamin? The psalm must reflect a time when both of the two entities, here called «Benjamin» and «Judah» were political realities.

That means a Davidic-post-Davidic time. For, in spite of Martin Noth[1], the «twelve tribe system» cannot be older than David; before David, Judah did not belong to «Israel»; the pre-Davidic amphictyonic Israel consisted of 10 tribes, as is clearly seen in the «Song of Deborah». The «twelve tribe system» is an ideological expression of the Davidic «whole state politics.»[2]

Now Albrecht Alt has taught us that the Davidic state from a constitutional point of view was a «united kingdom» «Judah and Jerusalem», or «Jerusalem and Judah», consisting of the tribal kingdom Judah and the originally Jebusite city-state of Jerusalem.[3] As the King of Judah he was elected by the chieftains of the clans; the city-state of Jerusalem was his personal property, the King's domain, hereditary in the royal family.

There is every reason to believe that this political state of things has had expression even in the ceremonial of the official religious festivals.

[1] Martin Noth, *Das System der zwölf Stämme Israels*, Stuttgart 1933.

[2] See the author's forthcoming article in the *Eissfeldt-Festschrift* 1958: «Rahelstämme» und «Leastämme».

[3] Albrecht Alt, *Die Staatenbildung der Israeliten in Paläestina*, Leipzig 1930, = *Kleine Schriften zur Geschichte des Volkes Israel* II, München 1953, pp. 1ff.

How have now these relations been incorporated and expressed in the official twelve tribe ideology? The city-state of Jerusalem had in pre-Davidic times belonged neither to Judah nor to Benjamin or to any other Israelitic tribe. Its wholly Canaanite origin and paramount Canaanite character were generally known. An Israelite «tribe Jerusalem» or «Jebus» could not therefore easily be constructed and put into the twelve tribe system, eventually on the place of the no longer existing Simeon or the imaginary Levi. It had in some or other way to be ideologically incorporated in one of the twelve tribes. Judah, however, was here impossible; that might include the danger of an effacement of the constitutional and — from the view point of the king — very important difference between Judah and Jerusalem. — But through the fall of the Saulides a place within the «system of twelve» had become free! There no longer existed in the political sense of this word, any tribe of Benjamin. The city-state of Jerusalem might without any political danger be reckoned as belonging to the tribe of Benjamin. Moreover, even a positive reason could lead to this theory. As David, in the constitutional theory, jure belli was the legitimate heir of Melchizedek, he played — as the son-in-law of Saul and the avenger of Ishba‘al (2. Sam. 4:2—12) — the legitimate heir of the Saulides as well; the tribe of Benjamin was his partrimony as well.

This is just the constitutional state and theory which is reflected in 68:28. «Benjamin» means here in fact the royal domain, Jerusalem. The terminology itself is rooted in political interests. But its form was excellent even from the viewpoint of religious and poetical romanticism. The motif of the youngest ($ça^e ir$) of the brethren, «the beloved of Yahweh» (Dtn. 33:12), who becomes the «ruler» of them all, a motif well known from all sorts of folk-lore, was especially apt to express the idea, from the view point of which David and his dynasty wanted themselves to be seen.

The order: Benjamin before Judah, although both of them are characterized as «rulers», is justified by the fact that «Benjamin» here represents the royal domain, the capital, the old city-state of Jerusalem.

So we must conclude: both Benjamin and Judah belong to the original text of 68:28. We have here to do with a real tricolon within a poem built up of regular bicola. — Why could not the poet here acquiesce in a bicolon, and thus break the regularity of the stanzas? — When historico-political realities and interests demanded that both «Benjamin» and Judah were expressly mentioned in a festal psalm, we are justified in thinking that the same special historico-political reasons stand behind the choice of the two other tribes mentioned: Zebulun and Naphtali as well. That means: the poet needed more than 1 bicolon to say what was to be said. As, however, the stanzas of his poem should contain 4 bicola, he did not want to break this scheme by giving this single stanza 5 bicola. So he choose to expand one of the bicola to a tricolon.

A similar intentional irregularity *may* be found in *Ex.* **15:1b —18**, the so-called «Song of Miriam». This poem too belongs to the psalm poetry. It is a regular cult psalm though not transmitted within the Psalter, but in connection with the Exodus legends. I take it for granted that this psalm cannot have originated from the time of Moses;[1] the allusion to the imigration and the (gradual) occupation of Canaan is too obvious. The poet's conception of the miracle at the Reed Lake[2] (*yam suf*) is dependent on the later form of the legends, see v. 8 «the waters were gathered together, the floods stood upright as a wall, the dephts were congealed in the heart of the sea», and compare 14:22 (P): «and the waters were a wall unto them on their right hand, and on their left». The last stanza v. 17— 18 mentions the sanctuary (*miqdåš*), «a holy place (*måkom*) for his abiding», that Yahweh has established on «the mountain of his inheritance», where He now «resides as King for ever». There can be no doubt that this is an allusion to the temple of Jerusalem and to Yahweh's royal festival, his enthronement festival there. Albright will not accept this interpretation of Yahweh's »mountain

[1] See *Der Achtundsechzigste Psalm*, pp. 73ff.

[2] Not «The Red Sea»! As the present author has demonstrated already in 1918, *yam suf* is not the Red Sea, but Birket et timsah at the eastern end of Wadi tumîlat; see Mowinckel, «'Sivsjøen' = Birket et-Timsah», [Dansk] Teologisk Tidsskrift, 1918, pp. 94ff. The present author can neither agree with Eissfeldt's opinion :Lacus Sirbonensis (*Baal Zaphon, Zeus Kasios und der Durchzug der Israeliten durchs Meer*, Halle 1932), nor with M. Noth's scepticism («Der Schauplatz des Meereswunders», *Eissfeldt-Festschrift*, pp. 181ff.)

of inheritance», so often found in O.T. in different variations; he says: «the home of Baʿal in the Canaanite epic, which was composed not later than 1 400 B.C., is said to have been ʿon the mountain of his inheritance'. It follows from this and other similar facts that there is no longer the slightest valid reason for dating the Song of Miriam after the thirteenth century B.C.»[1] This objection, however, has no validity. It is, of course, more than probable that the expression itself has been borrowed from Canaanite religious terminology. But as the Canaanites have used the expression about a definite mountain Mount Saphon, so the Israelites, of course, have applied it to a definite mountain, that to them was the inheritance and abode of *their* god, and that was above all Mount Zion. A similar application of a similar Canaanite expression on Mount Zion we have in Ps. 48:2.

According to the Massoretic verse-division *vv. 8, 9, 11, 15* are tricola. As for *v. 11* this is only due to an erroneous division; the monocolon v. 12 is obviously the parallel colon to v. 11c, giving the definite actual application of the general statement in 11c. But still there seems to be 3 isolated tricola among the 4 + 4 beat bicola (Mashal bicola) in the psalm.

What makes me a little suspicious is the fact that the text contains 43 Mashal cola,[2] that means, from the formal point of view: just one colon too little for 11 stanzas. The suggestion that 1 colon has been lost, seems not unlikely. *If so,* it would not

---

[1] See W.F. Albright, *Archaelogy of Palestine*, Pelican Books 1949, p. 233.

[2] V. 3b is too short; but as the right parallel to *ʾiš* (or *gibbor*, Sam cfr. G, BHK) seems not to be the naked *yhwh*, but his full name *yhwh ʾælohe çebaʾot*, the supposition does not seem unjustified that this have been the original text. Whatever might be the original meaning of this phrase, the Israelites have in O.T. times felt the nuance: the overmighty, the victorious, the Lord of mightfulness (omnipotence) as connected with it. See O. Eissfeldt, «Jahve Zebaoth» (*Miscellanea Academica Berolinensia*, 1950, pp. 126ff). V. Maag, *Jahwe's Heerscharen* (Separatdruck aus der Festschrift für Ludwig Köhler, «Schweizerische Theologische Umschau», Nr. 3/4, Bern 1950) arrives in another way at a similar result: *çebaʾot* is the integration of the mythical «Naturmächte» of Canaan, as an expression of the integration of the conception of Yahweh's omnipotence («Integration des Allmachtbegriffes»).

be quite impossible to take v. 9a as the «parallel» colon to v. 8c; the parallelism should, however, be a merely formal one, adding to v. 8 the new thought, the reaction of the enemies, which should then be described more in detail in the following stanza vv. 9b—10. A somewhat similar construction is in the stanza 18:25—28; v. 25 repeats the thoughts in v. 21, after the motivation in vv. 22—24, and belongs in so far logically to vv. 21—24; as the poet, however, wanted to elucidcate the thought by putting forward the general principle of Yahweh's just retribution, he added vv. 26—28, and made out of vv. 25—28 a new stanza. The same might be the case in Ex. 15:8—10; logically v. 9a is closely connected with v. 9b,c, but that does not exclude the possibility ot a metrical connection with v. 8. — If one admits the possibility of this suggestion, one also might admit that v. 14a metrically can be connected with v. 15. — It so, one might even admit the possibility that 1 colon has been lost before or after v. 14b — eventually before or after v. 15c. Then we should have 11 regular stanzas, two bicola to the stanza.

On the other hand: the separation of v. 9a from 9b—10 is, in fact, hard. It seems also natural to take v. 15a and 15b (Edom — Moab) as the parallel cola of one and the same bicolon, as TM does. If we take the vv. 8, 9, and 15 as original and intentional tricola, we shall at all events have a psalm with an irregular strophical construction. The stanza vv. 8—10 should consist of 2 tricola and 1 bicolon, vv. 13—15 of 2 bicola and 1 tricolon, all the other stanzas of 2 bicola each.

11.

Our investigation as far has led to the result that not only an isolated tricolon among regular bicola, but also isolated single cola amid bicola must be looked at with some suspicion. Very many of them disappear when considered in the light of text-critic, critical exegesis, and the formal demands of Hebrew poetry. In other cases we have to do with introductory or liturgical formulae extra metrum (§ 9).

We may take it for granted that not the single colon, but the bicolon (or sometimes: its offspring the tricolon) is the very building stone, the architectural unity of Hebrew poetry.

There exist, however, a few *monocolic poems*, in the Psalter represented by *111* and *112*, and *15:2—5a*. We have here to do with the special exceptions that confirm the rule. All these three belong to the latest psalm poetry.

Ps. 15 is materially a parallel to 24:3—4, a dramatic scene within the cultic procession up to the temple, playing before the temple gates, where the participants in the procession ask the priestly doorkeepers about the conditions for entering the holy place, *les torot d'entré*. See the author's *Psalmenstudien V*, pp. 58, 136; *Le Décalogue*, Paris 1927, pp. 141ff; *Offersang og Sangoffer*, pp. 156f. The answer to the question was given in accordance with the «decalogic tradition» the traditions about the basic commandments of the covenant. The influence not only of the material content but also of the form of this tradition is clearly seen in the fact that the answer comprises just 10 commandments, here, of cause, transcribed in the participle form: he that . . . etc. The traditional form of such commandments was the apodictic sentence. So the poet without difficulty could use just one colon to each of the 10 qualifications of the righteous man, who «shall never be moved» (v. 5), «who may ascend to the mountain of Yahweh» and «receive blessing from Him» (see 24:3,5). As an introduction the 10 cola have the 2 cola of the question in v. 1, and, likewise, the close consists of 2 cola; in v. 8c a *bâruk hu'* certainly is to be supplemented, cf. 24:5. We have a similar framework in Pss. 8 and 82, see *Johs. Pedersen-Festschrift* p. 253.[1]

But even here we see the «law of duality» at work: the single cola are often arranged according to the demands of the «thought rhyme»: vv. 2a ⊞ 2b (*holek ⊞ dorek*), 3b ⊞ 3c (*lere'ehu ⊞ 'al qerobo*), 4a ⊞ 4b (*nibzæ ⊞ yekabbed*), 5a ⊞ 5b (*kæsæf benæšæk ⊞ šohad*). Of course it was not possible to arrange just 10 definite commandments in that way; the poet did not «write» to express this private opinion, but for cultic liturgical use; he was not free to choose the 10 «commandments» according to the demands of a strong thought rhyme. In a poem, as this, it therefore does not make sence to speak of a

---

[1] What Gunkel (*Die Psalmen*, p. 12) says about a single bicolon at the end of the Pss. 17, 20, 27, 29, 33, 77, 82, 107 has no validity. See above p. 89 n. 1.

single colon at the end of the poem, as does Gunkel (*Die Psalmen übers u,erklärt*, Göttingen 1926, p. 12). The lines of Ps. 15 consist of single cola. The division of the verses in TM is in so far more correct than that of the printed lines in BHK. The basic importance of the bicolon is at work in the introduction v. 1.

Pss. 111 and 112 belong to the latest period of the Biblical psalm poetry, «the learned psalmody».[1]

111 is formally and, as to its content, a hymn of praise, as to its intention, however, an individual thanksgiving psalm; the «record» about the worshipper's distress and salvation, has been changed into a hymn of a more general content. The poet, a learned man, educated in the art of poetry, wanted at the same time to honour Yahweh by the artificial «alphabetic» form, and to show that he could master it even in an unusual and most difficult form, letting not every bicolon, but every colon begin with a new letter in alphabetical order. But then it became impossible to observe the rules of parallelism (thought rhyme). Each colon is to a large degree a unit of its own. But even here, as in 15, the traditional rule asserts itself. V. 10a and b are a pair of material parallels. See also vv. 7 (*'æmæt* ‡ *næ'ᵃamânim*) and 9 (*pedut* ‡ *berit*). In other cases, two cola make at least a «synthetic (correct: formal) parallelism» the latter continuing materially and syntactically the former, as in vv. 1, 2, 6.

112 is perhaps a work by the same poet. It is no psalm, but a «wisdom poem» of the same type as Ps. 1, describing the fate of the righteous and the wicked man respectively. As not seldom in wisdom poetry, the description begins as a word of blessing *'ašre*, thus giving the first letter of the alphabet. Of the 22 cola, the righteous gets the 19, the wicked only 3; it seems as if the author waited till the letter Resh gave him the catchword *râšâ'*. — Even here we see the influence of the old rule of parallelism; see vv. 1 (*yâre' 'æt yhwh* ‡ *bemiçwotâw hâfeç*) 2 (*zæra'* ‡ *dor*, might ‡ blessing), 6 (*le'olâm lo' yimmot* ‡ *lezekær 'olâm*), 10 (*kâ'âs* ‡ *šinnâw yahᵃroq*).

[1] See Mowinckel, *Offersang og Sangoffer*, pp. 368ff; «Psalms and Wisdom», *Supplements to Vetus Testamentum* Vol. III («*Rowley Festschrift*»), Leiden 1955, pp. 205ff.

In all these 3 poems the poet has had special reasons for his use of the single colon. They permit no conclusions as to the basic rules of Hebrew poetry, but just this one: that we here have to do with exceptions where the general rules again and again make themselves felt.

12.

What has been demonstrated in § 10 has shown us that a more sporadic use of tricolic verses within bicolic poems cannot be denied. We have found few of them that could be considered as certain. Among them I personally consider 68:28 as one of the most certain.

On the other hand, our investigation certainly has shown that there are a great many cases where an apparent tricolon is only due to inaccurate textual transmission. Not only the about 55 cases with wrong verse-division and inter-punctuation (§ 3), or the 28 where other text-witnesses show that TM has lost an original colon (§ 4), or that secondary elements have come in (§ 5), or where the alphabetic acrosticon proves disarrengements in the text (§ 6); but certainly also in many of the about 78 cases where exegetical considerations lead to the conclusion that TM is disarranged, secondarily expended, or fragmentary (§ 7).

Still there are many cases, especially among the ca. 80 dealt with in § 8, where many scholars will not be inclined to admit the weight of our arguments, and especially the weight of merely metrical arguments. And among these cases are also such as I myself admit that the arguments are not decisive; I have tried to express this by words as «may», «possibly», «probably» or the like. These cases are, therefore, uncertain.

But it has to be remembered that «uncertainty» is a two-edged sword. Uncertainty in these cases does not mean that there is a greater probability for the authenticity of the tricolon in question. Bearing in mind the history of transmission of TM, from the oral stage to the revised text of the Massoretes, there obviously are so many possibilities for errors in all minor matters, that TM in cases of motivated uncertainty scarcely can claim more than 50 : 50 in its favour. In metrical questions scarcely so much, at least, in my opinion. If one prefers to declare my text-critical «results» e.g. all the cases in § 7b, for uncertain, I should like to stress that this also can be put in this way: all those «tricola» are at best very uncertain. I admit that the choice between these two formulations to a rather high degree is a matter of temperament, but also of scientific conscience. I would not feel morally well by working with such «tricola» as if they were facts.

To sum up: in my opinion isolated tricola — or isolated single cola — are as a rule not found within a (mainly) bicolic psalm. There may, however, be some. We have mentioned above 68:28, and there may be others, especially among those dealt with in § 9. — Many of the apparent tricola, however, can by textual witnesses and/or exegetical considerations be proved to be due to errors in the transmission of the text. Very often this result is corroborated by metrical and strophical reasons. In other cases the question can be settled only on metrical grounds, which, of course, gives a much greater degree of uncertainty.

Additional Note.

The present author fully agrees with B. Duhm, that regular stanzas have been intended by the psalm poets with very few exceptions. Distinctive signs of intended stanzas are: a closer logical connection and formal parallelism between 2 or more stichs; refrains, as in 42/42, 46, 57, 67 (?three tristichs, refrain supplemented after v. 8 (Gunkel)?), 80, 99; even the alphabetic acrostichon, often an impediment at the forming of parallelism between the stichs (see above p. 99f), is sometimes used as a formal means of making the stanzas, as in 9/10, 37, 119, Lam. 1, 2, 3, 4.

In psalms as 3, 8^1, 9/10 (NB the acrostichon), 19B, 23, 28, 37 (NB. the acrostichon), 38, 42/43, 47, 48, 50, 57, 70, 73, 75, 83, 88, 98, 101, 103, 114, 116, 120, 121, 122, 123, 125, 126, 127, 130, 131^2, 132:11—18, 134, 141, Lam. 4, the regular distich stanzas to two bicola each, are so obvious that there can be no doubt that they

---

[1] Four distinct stanzas whithin a framework consisting of 1 bicolon at the beginning and the end respectively. See *Pedersen-Festskrift* pp. 251 ff.

[2] There is no reason to separate v. 3 from v. 2, as Gunkel (*Die Psalmen*) does, see *GTMMM* IV *ad loc.*

are intended, and that the few smaller irregularities can be considered as unimportant. In a great many others, as 4, 5, 7, 11, 12, 13, 14, 17, 27, 29, 35, 39, 40, 51, 54, 55, 58, 59, 60:3—7, 11—14, 62, 63, 64, 66, 67, 71, 72[1], 74, 75, 81:7—17, 84, 89, 90, 94, 97, 105, 106, 109, 118, 128, 133, 138, 139, 144, 145, 146, 148, we find that the clear distichs are so overwhelming, that we are justified in thinking that the exceptions in TM are due to later editing or textual corruption.

We have tristichs, stanzas to three stichs (bicola) each in 1, 2, 6, 22, 30, 31, 32, 36, 41, 56, 61, 69, 76, 77: 1—13, 82 (2 stanzas within a framework consisting of 1 stich at the beginning and end respectively; cpr. 8), 86, 92, 96, 102, 113, 115, 136, 140, 142, 143, 147, 149, Lam. 1, 2, 3.

Tetrastichs, stanzas to four stichs (bicola), we have in 18, 46, 49, 65, 68, 79, 80, 91, 124 (v. 5a variant to v. 4), 129, 135, 137.

Pentastichs: 20, 44 (?in TM 4 pentastichs and 2 tetrastichs), 99, 104, 132:1—10.

Heptastichs: 21, 33, 85.

Octostichs: 119.

In 42/43 the stanzas are arranged as «superstanzas», 5 distichs to each, separated from each other by the refrain, thus 3 decastichs. Likewise in 57, with 2 superstanzas, 3 distichs + 1 refrain stich to each.

Irregular stanzas we have e.g. in 44 (pentastichs and tetrastichs), 77, 107 (distichs and tristichs, originally perhaps distichs only), 136 and perhaps a few others.

Non-strophic are as far as I can see, 25, 34, 78, 111, 112 only. But even here the tendency to arrange the stichs into pairs, the «law of duality», often makes itself felt. — Also the poetical part of Job and great parts of the Wisdom of Sirach are written in basic stanzas, distichs.

As far as I can judge, the following psalms are written in Qinah metre: 4, 5, 14, 19B, 23, 28, 31, 32, 35, 36, 39, 40, 42, 43[2], 48, 52,

---

[1] 72:15 consists of 2 regular Qinah stichs (against Gunkel), s. above. p. 81.
[2] Also the refrain 42:6,12; 43:5 is written in regular Qinoth, see above p. 9, n. 2.

53 (= 14), 55, 62, 65, 69, 70, 71, 84[1], 98, 101, 110 (?), 113, 116, 119, 120, 121, 122, 123, 124, 125, 126, 128, 129, 130, 131, 133, 134, 136, 137, 142, 143 — in total 46 (45) psalms. The others are written in the Mashal metre. — The decision is, however, in some cases difficult, not least because of the unavoidable uncertainty of the text (see above p. 11ff).

There *may* be other more complicated metres among the uncertain samples of both the two above mentioned types, but they are, however, so far not recognizeable (cp. *StTh* VII, p. 85).

---

[1] Gunkel (*Die Psalmen*, p. 12) takes v. 13 as a «Sechser», a «final verse in a different metre». The verse can, however, be scanned as a Qinah, but with the caesura irregularily after *'asre*. But as the psalm is written in regular basic stanzas (s. above pp. 82f), there is reason to think that v. 13 is a liturgical refrain of the same sort as 2:12c (s. above p. 89f).

INDEX

The lists on p. 11 n. 1, p. 89 n. 1, and pp. 101–103 are not included.

www.ingramcontent.com/pod-product-compliance
Lightning Source LLC
Chambersburg PA
CBHW060429090426
42734CB00011B/2506